D1592715

Tree Gardens
Architecture and the Forest

Gina Crandell

PRINCETON ARCHITECTURAL PRESS — NEW YORK

Published by
Princeton Architectural Press
37 East Seventh Street
New York, New York 10003

Visit our website at www.papress.com.

Printed and bound in China
16 15 14 13 5 4 3 2 1 First edition

Editor: Nicola Bednarek Brower
Designer: Benjamin English

Special thanks to: Sara Bader, Janet Behning, Fannie Bushin, Megan Carey, Carina Cha, Andrea Chlad, Russell Fernandez, Will Foster, Jan Haux, Diane Levinson, Jennifer Lippert, Jacob Moore, Katharine Myers, Margaret Rogalski, Elana Schlenker, Dan Simon, Sara Stemen, Andrew Stepanian, Paul Wagner, and Joseph Weston of Princeton Architectural Press —Kevin C. Lippert, publisher

Library of Congress Cataloging-in-Publication Data
Crandell, Gina.
Tree Gardens : architecture and the forest / Gina Crandell.
p. cm.
Includes index.
ISBN 978-1-61689-121-3 (pbk. : alk. paper)
1. Forest landscape design. 2. Formal gardens—Design. 3. Formal gardens—Design—History. 4. Landscape architecture. I. Title.
SB475.9.F67C73 2013
712—dc23

2012029551

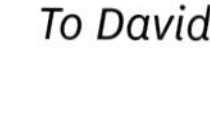

To David

Contents

Acknowledgments

Jane Gillette's delight at the idea of *Tree Gardens* got me started. I would like to thank my colleagues who reviewed the book proposal: Mira Engler, Iowa State University; Susan Herrington, University of British Columbia; Heath Massey Schenker, University of California, Davis; and particularly Linda Jewell, University of California, Berkeley, who invited me to be the Farrand Professor in 2007.

I would like to thank George Hargreaves for the lively design dialogue that his leadership shaped at the Harvard Graduate School of Design, which included many European landscape architects and out of which the seeds of this book were planted when I was teaching there from 1998 to 2002. I am also grateful to Dorothée Imbert for sharing her extensive knowledge of modern European practice when we taught together at GSD.

The long view of *Tree Gardens* developed thanks to Mikyoung Kim inviting me to teach history at the Rhode Island School of Design. I am grateful to Peter Walker for communicating his wisdom about the life of projects when he was editor-in-chief and I was senior editor of *Land Forum*.

I would like to thank colleagues and the landscape architecture offices included in this book for sharing photographs with me. I thank Nicola Bednarek Brower, senior editor at Princeton Architectural Press, for carefully reading my manuscript and escorting it through production.

Above all, I am grateful to my husband, David Roochnik, who has supported the entire journey, from conversations at the kitchen table to biking around parks in Europe.

Introduction

Imagine going for a walk in a temperate forest. A small opening in the canopy of trees follows the irregular outline of an unpaved parking lot that controls the number of visitors and sets the tone: this forest is managed at the lowest level of intervention so as not to harm the impression that it is natural. It's unkempt. It doesn't have distinct edges. As you walk into the forest, the trees you see are largely deciduous, interspersed with a few conifers. Because it is a regenerating forest, the tree trunks are mostly small, with occasional larger trees in between. Though this forest is constantly changing, change beyond the seasonal is not easily detected. Surprises are unlikely, with the exception of darting animals. The forest does indeed look natural. (Only trained eyes would perceive that it was logged a half century earlier.) As you walk the woods, you are left to your own thoughts, reliving the jarring conversation with a colleague at the office the day before, or wondering whether stock prices have fallen again. The comfortable "nature" we occasionally visit enables this personal reverie.

Now imagine something unexpected. Without a sign explaining why, the path takes you into a space nearly as large as a soccer field but circular and open to the sky. The circle is formed by a closely planted line of trees that shapes the edge of the woods beyond. Suddenly you are jolted out of your passive contemplation. You look more intently now. Questions arise. Who has intervened here? Why? Does this space, which is clearly intentional, have a functional purpose? Could it be purely aesthetic? The woods you just walked through seemed natural moments before, but now you wonder if it is. In fact, you begin to wonder what "natural" means.

It is the architecture of this intervention that is so surprising. You are so accustomed to encountering geometry in the forest at the service of industry that you are at first cynical about its purpose. But there is no evidence of industry here. It's a beautiful space. The contrast between the circular form and the apparent disorder of the regenerating forest sparks your interest. The round space becomes sculpture. Just as artist James Turrell's *Skyspace* works, it focuses on the sky. (Though the temptation is great, to put an object or sign in this space would negate this sculptural focus.) The geometric clearing increases your perception of the trees that form it and even more acutely of the forest itself. Intention provokes attention.

The circle also brings light to the forest, and the resulting natural processes encourage ecological understanding. At the base of the vertical trunks that form the perimeter, for example, a circle of fresh new woody growth appears. Botanical pioneers would take advantage of the light no matter what its shape, but the ring of growth makes this process more visible. Upon returning deep into the trees, you wonder how the forest came to be. The contrast between order and chaos, the intended and the untended, has heightened your engagement with the woods.

Tree Gardens investigates exemplary landscape designs that are based on a similar commingling of architecture—understood here as structures that are the product of human expression—and forest, consisting of close-growing trees that are thinned (naturally or purposefully) in the competition for resources. In the fifteen projects featured in the following chapters the forest inspires a variety of gardens located in the United States, Europe, and Asia.

Organized chronologically by time of design, the book begins with historic projects that have maintained a structure of trees over long time frames, dating back as far as the sixteenth century. Subsequent chapters discuss some of the most delightful contemporary works that express the bold exuberance of the forest at the same time as they acknowledge the significance of architectural intention in their success in celebrating natural processes. All still extant, the gardens acknowledge the impossibility of completion and the certainty of change that differentiates landscape architecture from building architecture. They illustrate a variety of ways tree structures, ranging from tens to thousands of trees, can form expressive spaces that heighten our understanding of nature.

1544 — LUCCA, ITALY

The Wooded Circle

TREE LIST[1]

Aesculus hippocastanum
Horsechestnut

Liriodendron tulipifera
Tulip Tree

Platanus × acerifolia
London Planetree

Quercus ilex
Holm Oak

Tilia platyphyllos
Bigleaf Linden

Ulmus sp.
Elm

Why is Lucca still the "city of the wooded circle," as it was described in the late nineteenth century? At that time, there was pressure to demolish the *mura*, its Renaissance walls built of earth and planted with trees, but the city decided to save both. An architectural appreciation of trees must have been so thoroughly associated with the early military and later civic identity of the walls that the city of Lucca has not only planted and felled many generations of trees on its mura, but also maintained for centuries their structure, consisting of same-species, similar-aged linear allées that circle the town.

Many European cities have fragments of their medieval or Renaissance walls tucked between newer buildings or interrupted by streets. Lucca is rare in preserving its complete landform, but it is particularly exemplary for maintaining the trees as an architectural configuration rather than simply replacing individual trees, which would have allowed the collective structure to slowly degrade. Since its military inception, the promenade has been segmented by bastions into eleven separately planted allées, which continue to be maintained as single-species, largely same-age structures.

Lucca's Roman footprint was in the center of a wide, vulnerable plain surrounded by mountains. Over the centuries the city's inhabitants built walls to protect themselves from intruders. Completed about 1265, medieval walls were built as high as twenty-one feet to keep out enemies scaling ladders. These tall, thin walls could not hold up to an attack by cannons, however, which were invented in the fifteenth century, nor accommodate the 130 cannons Lucca would acquire.

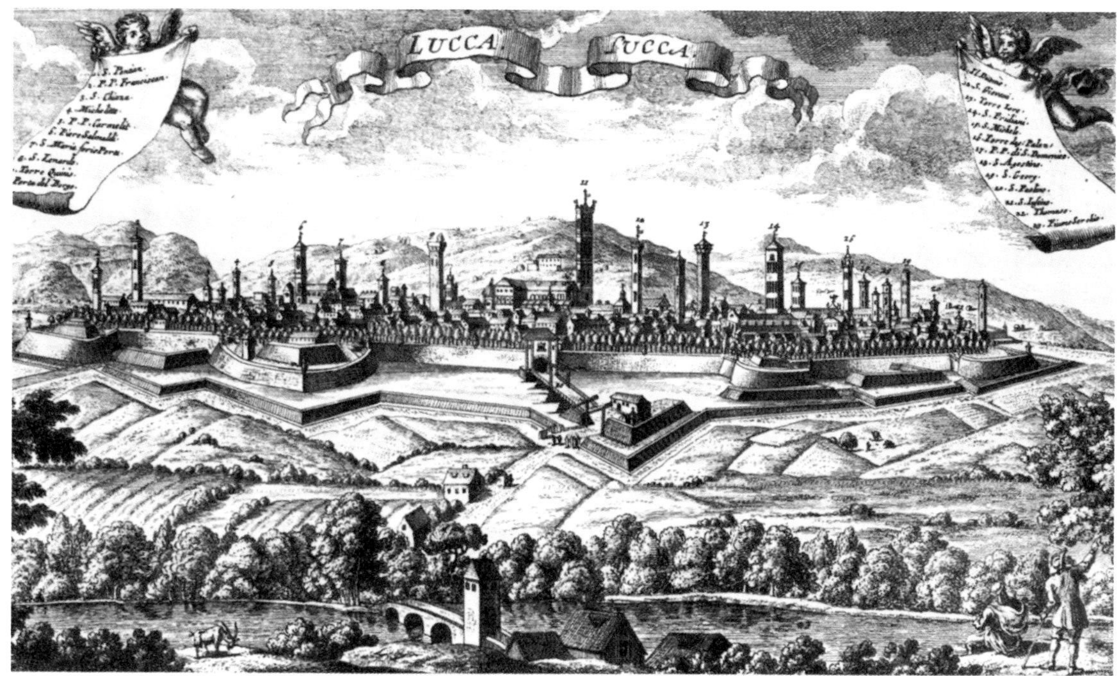

↓ This mid-eighteenth-century view of Lucca published by I. C. Leopold shows the massive landforms designed to defend the city. The trees planted on top of the ramparts in eleven allées, separated by pointed bastions, have become the promenade that encircles Lucca today.

↑ Lorenzo Nottolini's drawing of 1818 illustrates the tree-lined terraces on the inside of the embankment as well as the promenade at the top of the ramparts.

Therefore, from the early sixteenth to mid-seventeenth century, the medieval walls were transformed into the deep, spreading landforms we see today, with embankments inside to strengthen the walls and provide accessibility, as well as outward-protruding bastions for cannons and surveillance. These deep landforms both contained the city and extended its visibility outward.

The earliest trees were planted on the interior terraced or sloping embankments, behind the patrol way for the watch, as well as on the bastions that projected into a sterile zone where trees had been razed for better surveillance.[2] These first trees were fast-growing poplars whose primary function was to compact and consolidate the great mass of earth that made up the walls. Only two years after construction had begun, their status as public architecture was evident. "Francesco Bendinelli recounts their civic nature: 'The first planting soon made an excellent impression, because the people were all greatly pleased with the agreeableness and ease of taking an airing, just as if they were at their own villas.'"[3] In an early illustration, carriages can be seen at the top of a landform where soldiers are also guarding the cannons.

↓ On the inside of the embankment, strollers once gathered on the tree-planted terraces while spectators were seated in the amphitheater.

Construction of the fortification was completed by the middle of the seventeenth century, although maintenance remained a costly and labor-intensive endeavor. For example, trees along the curtain wall embankments and bastions had to be regularly felled and replaced. By the mid-eighteenth century, issues of security had waned, and the landforms

↑ The inside embankment today where trees were first planted to consolidate the earth. A ramp leads up to the tree-lined promenade.

were mostly used for pleasure. City gates were left open at night. Never having been used, the cannons were all removed by the end of the eighteenth century. The trees were increasingly valued for their collective beauty and the social space they created. The wooded circle was recognized as a public asset; it had become a promenade.

The final transformation of the planted walls to public architecture was the work of Maria Luisa, Bourbon Duchess of Lucca, who, in 1818, commissioned architect Lorenzo Nottolini (1787–1851) to create a planting plan with broad-leafed trees that were esteemed for the shade and structure they provided to a pleasant carriage drive or walk on the walls during the summer months.[4] Twin lines of plane trees were planted on either side of the pathway, which was flat and well suited for strolling. The parapet that had protected the patrol way was lowered to provide a better view of the countryside, and by the mid-nineteenth century marble benches had been installed along the promenade at regular intervals. The Santa Maria military barrack was demolished in 1840 to make way for the Caffè delle Mura, a final sign that the fortified ring had become a place for recreation and socializing.

The wooded circle is on the ridge of the earthwork, between the densely built city and the wide expanse that was historically left unbuilt for defensive reasons. For people on the circuit today, seeing outsiders approach the city is no longer a duty but a pleasure. The perched viewer looks both into the dense fabric of the city and out across the open expanse of the now smaller sterile zone, over the far trees and across the expanded city to a distant mountain ridge. The reverse is also true: Lucca and its ramparts are seen from afar, just

↓ A new generation of closely planted plane trees proposed by Nottolini in the nineteenth century reinforced the social nature of the promenade.

↑ The sterile zone that was left unbuilt in the sixteenth century for defensive reasons is maintained today for historical reflection and simply for the view.

as they have been for centuries. These days, inhabitants and visitors bicycle and walk along the ramparts all day, and in the evening, when the promenade is lit.

Some of the trees that were specified by Nottolini's plan of 1818 have recently been replanted. In one allée are four young rows of pyramidal, closely planted plane trees identifiable by their variegated, exfoliating bark ranging in color from cream to olive green. They cast individual shadows, since they are still too small for their canopies to become one mass. In an adjoining allée, a much older generation of plane trees forms a large, open, wide-spreading structure. Visitors are impressed by the historical and temporal qualities that the contrast between these two generations of plane trees confers. These are familial generations—grandparents and grandchildren—embodying the difference between older plants and young ones, while affirming the continuity of affection for the allées by Lucca's citizens.

↓ Replanted following Nottolini's plan, at the end of the twentieth century another generation of closely planted plane trees forms an allée on the promenade.

↘ An adjoining allée of a much older generation of plane trees reminds the visitor of Lucca's history.

↑ An aging generation of tulip trees forms this allée on the south side of the circuit.

The different generations of trees speak to Lucca's history, from its military past to its present appeal to visitors. It is a rare gift—generations of trees planted by generations of Lucchesi. There are other ages and species of allées elsewhere around the circuit. Many of them were planted by people no longer living. Some of the trees might even have been there when the city's cannons were installed on the bastions. It is the repetition of the structure—allées—that incites the stroller to notice these two variables—age and species—with their nuanced differences, such as leaf shape, bark ridges, and fruits. Frequent visitors today know where they are in the city without a map because the allées themselves are so identifiable.

Walking on the south side of the circuit toward the east, the stroller is confronted with three allées of different species. One is a double row of very large, closely planted tulip trees with their upright posture and tulip-shaped leaves (see image above). Most of the aging trees were planted about twenty feet on center. The next allée is graced with closely planted large old horsechestnuts with their distinctive palms holding six leaves, their branches opening up the platy bark of their trunks. The third allée is formed by double rows of tall, stately old lindens with their upright, fissured trunks and gracefully drooping branches. These contrasting qualities of species become more apparent when one walks the whole circuit. After the San Salvatore bastion, the east segment is an allée of very large and closely planted oaks.

The north side of the circuit is largely planted with lindens that vary in size from allée to allée. One segment is an astonishing double row of lindens whose trunks are more than three feet in diameter, twenty feet apart, and more than sixty feet tall. Others are

An old generation of horsechestnuts

→ A narrow, middle-aged allée of linden trees on the promenade is above the old city to the left and the open plain on the right.

middle-aged. Hundreds of lindens have been planted recently in another section, with their dense, pyramidal canopies standing on youthful slender trunks.

Even though these allées follow earlier generations of trees, they are not planted based on the strict preservation of Nottolini's or any other plan. They are, however, carefully evaluated. Today the Opera delle Mura di Lucca manages the historic site, listing nearly three thousand trees in its database that have been mapped, inventoried, monitored for disease, and that are vigilantly observed. Those who have made decisions about these allées over the years have understood that the presence of various generations of trees demonstrates to people that there is a long history here, which is more important than precise historical imitation. Most importantly, they have recognized that the trees' social and aesthetic value lies in maintaining the structure of allées of distinct species.

→ These more recently planted linden trees on the promenade cast individual shadows.

1549 — FLORENCE, ITALY

Boboli Garden

Niccolò Tribolo

AS PAINTED BY GIUSTO UTENS, 1599

TREE LIST

Abies alba
European Silver Fir

Cupressus sempervirens
Italian Cypress

Laurus nobilis
Bay Laurel

Quercus ilex
Holm Oak

Cosimo de' Medici's Boboli Garden at the Pitti Palace in Florence, Italy, was designed in the mid-sixteenth century, about the same time that the city of Lucca began constructing its earth embankments. Court artist Niccolò Tribolo (1500–1550) received the commission in 1549, and the planting of trees started immediately.[1] Flemish painter Giusto Utens (d. before 1609) painted the garden a half century later, in 1599. While the painting is not a technically accurate depiction of Tribolo's design, Utens had seen its construction completed and its trees matured. In order to glorify his patron, the artist likely exaggerated the perfection of the garden, represented by the painting's omniscient point of view. Nevertheless his depiction provides a powerful framework for acknowledging the conception of the garden as art and the forest as architecture. Revised and enlarged nearly beyond recognition over the centuries, the Boboli Garden of Utens's painting no longer exists today, so it is to the painting that we look for understanding. Here we are introduced to the garden's orthogonal compartments, the quincunx, and the orchard.

It took the confidence of the Renaissance to think of the garden as art. In sixteenth-century Italy, privately owned former hunting grounds, which were already tamed by enclosing walls and supplied with aqueducts, were being transformed into large-scale gardens with rivers and wooded areas. The Italian word for forests, *boschi*, came to be also applied to groves of trees in these gardens, which were often arranged in geometric configurations, such as the quincunx.

A quincunx is defined as a grouping of five, with one point at each corner of a square or rectangle and one in the center. The quincunx planted with trees was inspired by classical literature and employed in many Renaissance gardens: Cicero wrote about King Cyrus of Persia, who had planted trees in this configuration. In Utens's painting, trees are shown in quincuncial arrangements at the top of the hillside, above the bowl and pool. Over a large area, the quincunx is essentially one grid placed over another, which adds complexity to the visitor's experience. Diagonal lines of trunks and alleys are emphasized. At the same time there is an occasional perception of disorder when the viewer is looking between the rows of trunks. A stroll within the geometry of trees results in an appreciation of both the bounty of nature and the spatial qualities of architecture.

Utens's paintings of sixteenth-century Medici gardens depict not only the bold idea of the forest as art but also exemplify the problematic concept of the garden as a static image. Far from being untouched, the U-shaped bowl at the center of the Boboli Garden that was created out of a natural hollow had also been quarried for stone, constituting a very early landscape adaptation of a mined site.[2] In what must have been a dramatic transformation of the former mine, *boschetti*, small forests, were planted over many decades in square compartments around the *prato*, or lawn, at the base of the hollow.[3]

Giusto Utens's Boboli Garden of 1599 is subdivided into compartments where *boschetti*, or small forests, of a single species, reveal the underlying order of nature.

↑ Detail of the U-shaped bowl planted with boschetti

In addition to illustrating various spacing schemes, Utens painted these forest compartments with different textures and shades of green to differentiate species. The tallest trees are firs planted at the base and extending to the top of the hollow. Vertical cypresses hold the structure of the corners. Large holm oaks curve around the bowl on the ridge, and smaller laurel trees cross the bowl from ridge to ridge.[4]

These compartments of various tree species transform the idea of the forest into a work of art and a celebration of botany. Nature in the Renaissance was interpreted as a collection of raw materials—plants, stone, water, and land—to be shaped and organized by art.[5] Nature was also thought to have an underlying order that was expressed by mathematics.[6] What we see when the forest is abstracted into compartments, as shown here, is a representation of this order. Unlike buildings of stone that follow mathematical proportions, the trees in these geometrical spaces constantly change. They grow, reproduce, and die, but since they cannot move, the very geometry of their placement both challenges natural processes and expresses nature's underlying order.

Garden architects of the Italian Renaissance recognized the compelling liveliness of the relationship between art and nature. One was always competing to overwhelm the other. When we look at Utens's painting today, it would seem at first glance that art surpasses nature here (if nature exists in the painting at all) because of its overwhelming geometry and perfection. But when we think of what the actual Boboli Garden might have looked like to someone walking there in 1599, we can begin to appreciate how dynamic the contest between art and nature really was: The boschi would have had nearly a half century of growth when Utens painted them. The individuality of a single tree would have been absorbed into the collective structure of each compartment. The architecture of the groves would have been felt in structural masses as well as in the repetition of trunks celebrating nature's geometrical order. Some of the trees may have died.

The visitor would have noticed a vivid contrast between the heavy shade in the holm oaks compartments, as opposed to the groves of smaller laurel trees. The orchards would have become heavy with fruit, celebrating the fecundity of nature's processes. Fragrance would have abounded when the orchards were in bloom, or when the aroma of the bay was released from the leaves. In winter the branches of the deciduous compartments would have been seen as a sculptural mass, with light reaching the ground. The silver of the fir trees and the verticality of the cypress trees would have stood out prominently from the broadleaved compartments. In so many ways, the architecture of the garden would have dramatized the effects of nature.

The orthogonal grove is surely also a legacy of agriculture. Fruit trees had long been one of the three basic elements of gardens. In order for trees to produce the desired fruit, they are planted in rows that form grids and are spaced at distances that anticipate a plentiful harvest. Multiple compartments of fruit trees, conventionally planted

Detail showing orchards of fruit trees, running downhill from the fort to the street. The protruding rectangle on the left illustrates Cosimo's orchard of dwarf fruit trees.

planted in rows among grass or low herbs, can be seen on the left side of Utens's painting, running downhill from the fort to the street. The Mediterranean climate is ideal for fruits and nuts, and Italian Renaissance gardens were often planted with trees such as almond, apple, apricot, cherry, fig, filbert, lemon, orange, peach, pear, pistachio, plum, pomegranate, and walnut. The protruding rectangle further to the left represents Cosimo's orchard of dwarf fruit trees, the first illustrated instance of such trees and a celebration of the early pride of botanical management.[7]

Utens may have painted the garden at the most opportune time to emphasize its architectural structure. Many decades later, as processes of aging advanced, trunks would have become chunky and branches uneven. More trees would have been lost, and if maintenance had been neglected, there would have been little evidence left of the geometrical compartments. Instead, as often happens, the design of the garden was largely lost to revisions.

Early in the seventeenth century, the trees that had been planted following Tribolo's design would have been fifty to eighty years old, past maturity and beginning to degrade. Rather than replacing them in compartments on the sloping hillside, the U-shaped bowl at the center of the garden was transformed into a theater, first with wooden seats, then since 1637, in stone.[8] At the same time, the park tripled in size with an appendage to the west that is spatially unrelated to the garden Utens painted. A dominating axis of cypresses, the Viottolone, extends the length of the addition. At the turn of the nineteenth century, French alterations to the garden mimicked the modern style of the time—ironically, the English garden—further altering the original design.[9]

In 1637 the sloping bowl, once quarried for stone and later planted with forest compartments, was returned to stone in the form of an amphitheater that remains in the garden today.

1661 — VERSAILLES, FRANCE

Versailles

André Le Nôtre

TREE LIST

Acer sp.
Maple

Aesculus hippocastanum
Horsechestnut

Corylus colurna
Hazel

Fagus sylvatica
European Beech

Fraxinus excelsior
European Ash

Juglans sp.
Walnut

Platanus sp.
Planetree

Prunus sp.
Wild Cherry

Quercus sp.
Oak

Salix caprea
Goat Willow

Tilia sp.
Linden

Ulmus sp.
Elm

The boschetti, or tree compartments, of the Italian Renaissance garden grew into *bosquets* in the seventeenth-century French garden: walled thickets of trees, delineated by axes that merged vast gardens with existing forests at the scale of landscape. The classical French garden was a synthesis of geometry and forestry.

Versailles is one of the most influential gardens because it became a model of spatial organization not only for gardens but also for cities all over the world. During the reign of Louis XIV (1638–1715), André Le Nôtre (1613–1700), the park's designer, drove its central axis more than five miles into the distant forest, creating the so-called Grand Prospect and erasing the boundary between garden and the regional landscape. Much has been written on the four-hundred-year history and design of Versailles. The focus here is on the garden's living structure, continuing to endure as the destructive force of time wreaks havoc on it.

How does one maintain the thick wooded interior and the architecturally walled exterior of bosquets? The life span of many temperate trees is about one hundred years. Various factors of management include decisions about when to fell, cost considerations, repairing damage caused by storms and disease, and the sheer difficulty of felling and replanting tens of thousands of trees. The planting cycles at Versailles, where planting takes about twenty years, have generally begun in roughly one-hundred-year intervals: during the 1660s, 1770s, 1860s, and 1990s.[1]

The First Planting, 1661–82

The forests and wetlands that became the garden of Versailles were formerly hunting grounds whose heavy soils, saturated with water, were not suitable for farming. In 1661, after seeing Le Nôtre's work at Vaux-le-Vicomte, the twenty-three-year-old Louis XIV engaged the forty-eight-year-old landscape designer at Versailles. Construction of Le Nôtre's plans began as early as 1668, and the work continued for decades. In 1682 the king, his court, and the government were established at Versailles. Louis XIV himself revised the park many times during his reign of more than fifty years.

The garden's main axes were derived from corridors that had been cut into dense woods to provide access for travel and hunting. The corridors and wooded thickets that had existed at Louis XIII's former hunting park roughly corresponded to the area of Le Nôtre's design for the Petit Parc, the 190-acre garden close to the château. There he transformed the thickets into fourteen bosquets that give vital structural form to the park's spatial voids of parterres, pools, and allées. The axes separating the bosquets became allées for strolling and fêtes, and the bosquets themselves became destinations.

The perimeters of these thickets were pruned and fenced into vertical walls. With a scale and density much more like city blocks than a forest, Le Nôtre's bosquets nevertheless captured a quality familiar

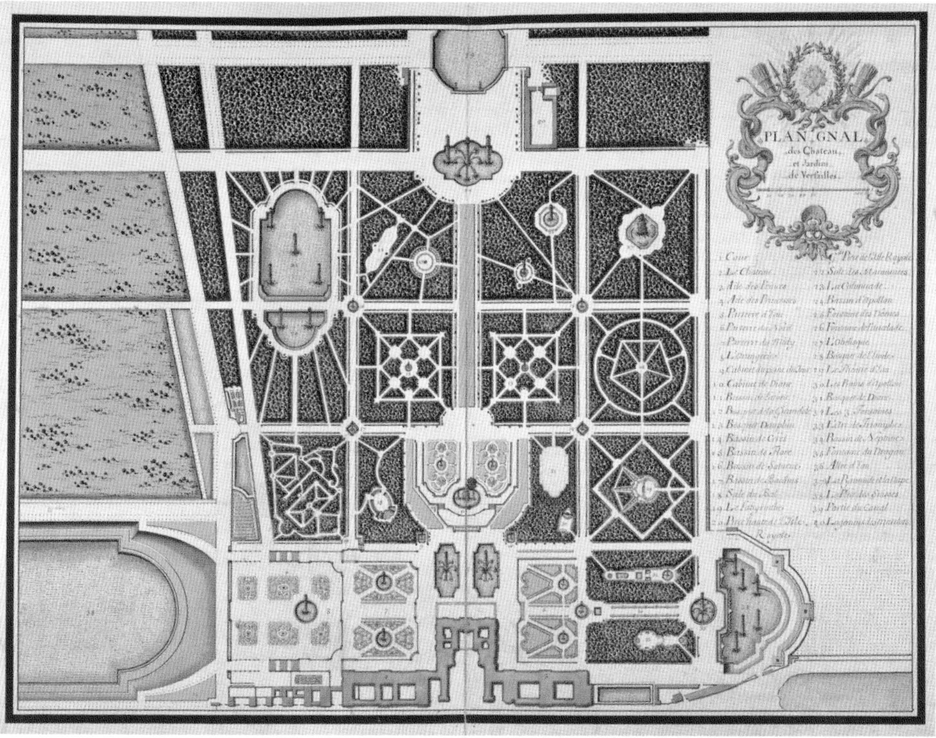

↑ Jean Chaufourrier's (1679–1757) watercolor from 1720 illustrates Le Nôtre's plan of the Petit Parc showing the fourteen bosquets in front of the château, indicated by dark forest with paths to interior spaces. Note the fine lines of the palisades surrounding each bosquet.

← This intersection of bosquets illustrates the establishment of architectural walls, consisting of closely planted trees that are pruned and reinforced by lattice fencing, and the palisades outside them that heighten the experience of discovery within.

to the exploration of dense woods—a sense of adventure. Elms and horsechestnuts planted along avenues and allées surrounding the bosquets added spatial layers to heighten the discovery within. To further raise curiosity about the interior, Le Nôtre thickened the perimeter and threshold of each bosquet, much like the walls and gates of a building. To achieve this impenetrability, he designed palisades—high, pleached hedges of closely spaced trees—that operated as a dense frame around the woods, opening at the point of entry. Palisades were often constructed of hornbeam trees, but he also planted thousands of oak, chestnut, beech, ash, walnut, wild cherry, and sycamore trees to frame and strengthen the bosquets.

Le Nôtre's design for the Grand Parc, which extends beyond the Petit Parc, projected orthogonal and radiating axes into the countryside encompassing thirty-four farms and six villages and covering over thirty-seven thousand acres. The central space of the Grand Parc is opened by the Grand Canal, bordered by tall trees, formerly elms, now replaced with lindens. Tens of thousands of trees were brought in from Flanders and other regions of France, and the reforestation continued for decades. According to records of expenditures for Versailles, in the autumn of 1686 alone, "one million 585 thousand small hornbeams, 148 thousand goat willows, 9 thousand maples and hazels, 8,400 elms, 255 sycamores, and 85 thousand small two-year-old elms were transported to Versailles from Lyon and Rouen."[2]

The Grand Prospect at Versailles extends for miles, illustrating the synthesis of garden and landscape, geometry and forestry. The bosquets of the Grand Parc in the distance frame the Grand Canal. Young trees forming the Allée du Tapis Vert in the Petit Parc, at the center of this view, were planted after 1994 to re-establish the downward gradation as one looks to the horizon.

At the time of Le Nôtre's death in 1700, the trees had reached the ideal proportions that he had envisioned: high palisades surrounding bosquets of trees that were not yet tall enough to obscure the main axes and perspective distance. Though the Petit Parc was a constantly changing, living structure, it had reached the peak moment of Le Nôtre's vision. Louis XIV held elaborate fêtes that the garden had been designed to highlight. Celebrations lasted for days and extended into the night when lighted earthenware pots, hung in the boughs, illuminated the trees. Feasting was interspersed with spectacles such as plays, ballets, equestrian parades, and fireworks.

The First Replanting, 1774–86

The old trees planted during Louis XIV's reign were lighted for the last time for the marriage of Louis XV's grandson in 1770. Louis XV had little means or interest to maintain the gardens. With the exception of a partial replanting of thousands of trees in 1747, in response to unusually cruel frosts and devastating storms, the majority of trees were simply left alone and altered by time until the damage was irreparable. Many trees became too tall to be pruned by gardeners balanced on

↓ Hubert Robert's *Vue du Tapis Vert à Versailles en 1775* illustrates the felling of trees for the first replanting of the Petit Parc.

↑ Old linden palisades along the Grand Canal, which was planted with elm palisades during Le Nôtre's time.

scaffolding. Seeking the sun, they spread their branches out of the vertical walls of the palisades and bosquets that Le Nôtre had designed. It was only when Louis XVI (1754–1793) took power in 1774 that the bosquets were reestablished.

The felling of trees in the Petit Parc created a spatial dislocation and a structural absence that can be seen in the *Vue du Tapis Vert à Versailles en 1775* (View of the Tapis Vert in 1775) by Hubert Robert (1733–1808) (see page 34). The Tapis Vert, the green carpet, is the long panel of grass on the central axis in the Petit Parc. The Grand Canal in the Grand Parc is the only recognizable feature in the painting, retaining its bosquets of elms along both sides. In the foreground, great trees lie among statues that look lost without the groves of trees that formerly framed them. Robert took picturesque advantage of the Grand Prospect in the distance by contrasting it to the sublime chaos of devastation in the foreground. The king and Marie Antoinette are surveying the destruction of the garden, a decade before their own destruction by the people of France. Children play on an improvised seesaw made from a tree once specified by Le Nôtre.

During the two winters it took to cut down the old trees, questions arose about how to replant the garden. Should the species to be planted be those found in French woods or new exotic ones imported from around the globe? Could the work of art be seen separately from the monarchy who had ordered it? Should the English landscape garden, which was becoming fashionable and thought to represent enlightenment, become a model? Could the historical importance of the garden design at Versailles be anticipated even though it had come to be considered passé? Issues of economy ultimately led to a partial replanting that maintained Le Nôtre's organization and abandoned the idea of exotic species.

In 1789 the royal family fled Versailles. After the revolution, there was talk of plowing under the garden, selling the trees, and using the land for farming. Instead, the park was officially opened up to the public and made more productive: parterres were turned into kitchen gardens, and fruit trees were planted near the château and around the Grand Canal.

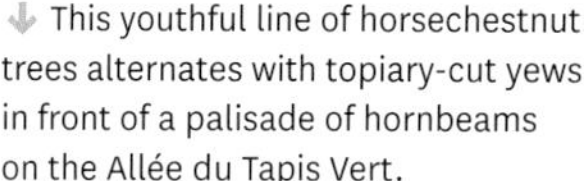

↓ This youthful line of horsechestnut trees alternates with topiary-cut yews in front of a palisade of hornbeams on the Allée du Tapis Vert.

The Second Replanting, 1860–86

By the time the trees planted under Louis XVI's direction had achieved maturity, the entire château and garden were in a state of disrepair. Versailles was regarded as little more than an obsolete artifact of absolutism. Napoleon III initiated the second replanting beginning in 1860 with diagonal avenues of lindens followed by the planting of plane trees along the cross paths. A hurricane in 1870 devastated old avenues. The Tapis Vert did not receive new chestnut trees until 1876, during part of a general replanting. Alterations of this time simplified and refined Le Nôtre's bosquets.

↑ In two hours on one of the last days of the twentieth century, 10,000 trees became victims of a devastating storm.

↗ The linden palisade at the far end of the Grand Canal is being inspected from a basket atop the shining telescopic arm of a maintenance vehicle.

The Third Replanting, ongoing since 1991

In the twentieth century, Versailles became the world's garden. The first visitors were soldiers stationed there during World War I. Today ten million sightseers can be expected each year. The park is surrounded by urban development with a vocal public constituency to protect Versailles, both locally and globally. Nostalgia combined with the fact that people simply love venerable old trees long prevented everyone from accepting the fact that many of the huge old trees again needed to be felled. By the 1960s, many trees planted in the nineteenth century were weak from age and disease. The bosquets had grown so tall that they completely obscured the effects of Le Nôtre's Grand Prospect.

Reluctance to fell further was overcome by the unsentimental power of a storm in 1990 that brought down 1,300 trees. Consequently, a committee of experts developed a restoration plan. For the Petit Parc they agreed to restore Le Nôtre's design to the period of 1700–1715, when it was at its peak. The felling and replanting program that they planned would take more than twenty years.

On December 26, 1999, however, nature dealt another devastating blow to Versailles: In two hours, 10,000 of the park's 350,000 trees were destroyed by a storm. The tall canopies of the bosquets that had lined the grand axis from the château lay crumpled, looking like the remains of a battle. More than 90 percent of the trees lost were more than two hundred years old. Every space was affected, and all kinds of tree species were down.

Oaks, chestnuts, ashes, and lindens are now among the hundreds of trees that are being felled every winter, bosquet by bosquet, in the Grand Parc. At the same time, thousands of slender hornbeam,

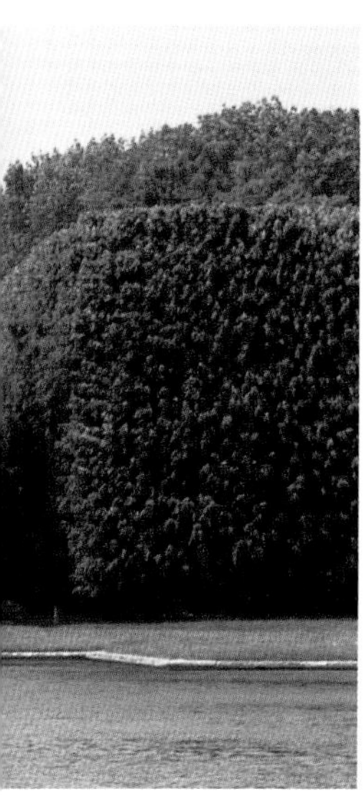

field maple, beech, linden, larch, and North American tulip trees are replacing the vegetal architecture that formed the bosquets in previous generations.

How can one comprehend this work of landscape art as historical when it is composed of a material that must be replaced every century, renews itself every spring (if not every day), and grows to mask the horizon if not checked? It is no longer possible to experience the Versailles of Louis XIV. Versailles is now a tourist site, and there is not one tree left planted by Le Nôtre. Nevertheless, a scrupulous restoration of the Petit Parc provides visitors an experience that is distinctly of the twenty-first century while also transporting them back to 1715, the time of the park's apotheosis. The tree list, while expressing a contemporary return to native species, will also be more diversified within plantations to guard against the potential loss of structure from disease. The selection of species for design purposes has always been important. The specification of trees with differing growth rates, for example, is now producing not only greater diversity but also bosquets that thicken more quickly. Trees with slower long-term growth rates may mature to the height specifications proposed centuries ago by Le Nôtre without pruning.

Today the palisades of trees (as well as topiary) are regularly pruned with the help of machines that use lasers, allowing an unprecedented degree of precision. It is already possible to begin seeing the Petit Parc around the château taking the shape it had at the time of Le Nôtre's death. That classic form, however, now expresses significantly revised thinking about both governance and ecology.

↓ Linden bosquets form a stage for ten million visitors to Versailles each year.

1858 — NEW YORK, NEW YORK

Central Park Mall

Frederick Law Olmsted

TREE LIST

Ulmus americana
American Elm

Ulmus procera
English Elm

When Louis XVI set out to repair the bosquets at Versailles in 1774, reports of the fashionable English landscape garden were in the air. Eighteenth-century English gentry were reading classical texts and traveling to Italy on the Grand Tour. There they were impressed by picturesque ruins, such as Emperor Hadrian's first-century villa and the sixteenth-century Medici villa gardens that were degraded by time. Painted landscapes of pastoral and wild scenery framed with deep perspectives of trees made untended, seemingly untouched nature into art. The gentry returned to England with a new appreciation of beauty as they carried with them memories of landscapes and, in some cases, painted renditions by Claude Lorrain and Salvator Rosa that would become visual models for the design of English landscape gardens.

The English at that time considered landscapes that were designed to look naturalistic more sensible than those expressing the rigid geometry that was thought to underlie nature during the Renaissance.

↑ English landscape gardens were extensively graded to create the undulating lines of ponds and sheared hills, planted with trees, as exemplified by Capability Brown's redesign of Petworth Park in 1750, photographed in 1983.

More importantly, they linked the idea of freedom to the absence of (French) geometry. They understood that park scenery, constructed on private estates with undulating sheared hills and crowned with closely planted clumps of trees, was not, in fact, natural but artificial. After all, they had witnessed the removal of small villages and agricultural fields that accompanied the gardens' construction.

When Frederick Law Olmsted (1822–1903) traveled to England in 1850, he was deeply impressed by the first designed park that he visited, Birkenhead Park near Liverpool, not only because it was accessible to the public but also because of its naturalistic scenery. In the winding paths and constantly varying surfaces, with dense planting on steep slopes and open lawns, he saw its capacity to relax the mental faculties and to offer freedom of movement. Olmsted was a social visionary. He believed that democratic institutions—libraries, hospitals, and parks—could equalize opportunity and incubate good citizens. During the nineteenth century, he would employ the landforms, groves, and vast spaces that characterized the English landscape garden in American public parks.

Olmsted's reputation for creating beautiful landscapes was secured with the construction of Central Park. Throughout the park, with the exception of the Mall, he aimed for two primary landscape effects. One offered the pleasing uncertainty of distance through the creation of an undulating meadow of turf that was surrounded by and disappeared into the shadows of masses of trees. This he contrasted to the second effect, the tighter spaces and rugged ground exemplified by the wild garden he designed in Central Park, now called the Ramble. At the time of the park's creation, New Yorkers would not have doubted that either of these landscapes was as synthetic as the bosquets at Versailles. After all, they, too, had seen the massive transformation that had taken place. Today, however, few would guess the depth of the artifice. Once the memory of construction fades and natural processes take over, intention becomes invisible. In a naturalistic landscape, this process is accelerated.

Thirty years after the construction of Central Park, Olmsted was commissioned to review the condition of the park's trees in response to what he and others had seen as a negligent lack of thinning due in part to the objections of an earnest public for the protection of their trees. He reported his findings in "Observations on the Treatment of Public Plantations, More Specifically Relating to the Use of the Axe" (1889), for the Park Commissioners of New York.[1] One striking word in the title is "plantations," a term that is now so unfavorably linked to commercial forestry that it is hard to recover Olmsted's pride in using it to describe the woodlands of Central Park. Yet Olmsted's appreciation of the word is revealing, as it acknowledges the human role in making a garden of trees, regardless of whether or not it is expressed in geometry or naturalistic forms or whether it is for the purpose of harvest or for the public's enjoyment.

In the report, Olmsted expresses his understanding of life cycles and the way plants grow to take advantage of light and space. He advocates for the close planting and thinning of masses of trees:

> It will be observed that all agree that in good practice trees are planted originally much closer than it is desirable that they should be allowed to grow permanently, and that, from every well-planted large body of trees, some are removed every year up to at least eighty years.... We should ourselves be classed with that which favors the less uniform use of the axe, and which believes in sometimes sacrificing more of the chances for long and perfect development of trees to the result of a more playful disposition and greater variation of companionship of them. We should, more than some, guard in thinning against making any tree individually conspicuous.

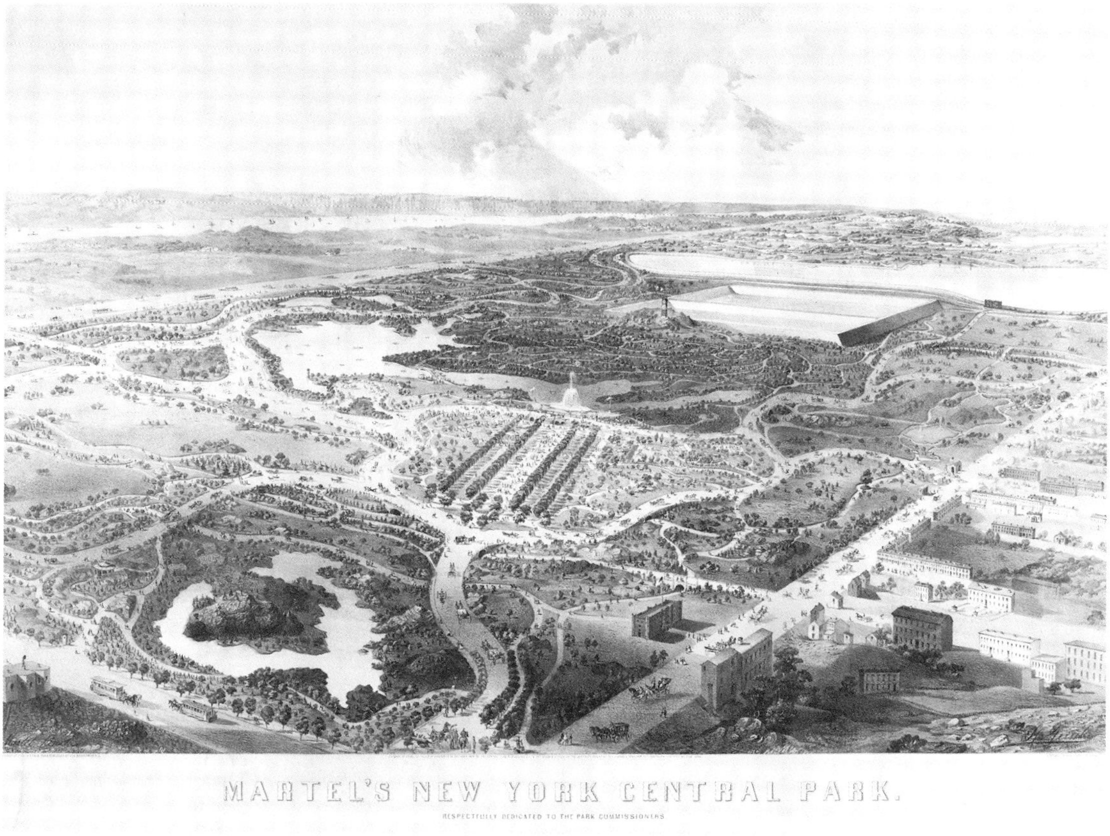

↑ Olmsted's alignment of the Mall's elms is exaggeratedly depicted at the center of this 1864 lithograph of Central Park.

↓ Central Park Mall when the elms were first planted

Familiar aerial photographs of Central Park now illustrate the vast canopy that has grown up, opening only to lawns and lakes. The general history and design of the park is well documented. My main focus in this chapter will therefore be what is now referred to as the Mall: the rare example of geometrically arranged trees planted within a naturalistically designed landscape of groves and glades.

Olmsted and Calvert Vaux's winning design for Central Park, the 1858 Greensward Plan, proposed the southern half of the park to be structured by two major vistas that intersect at one of the highest outcrops in Manhattan, aptly named Vista Rock. One was a line of sight that extended north from near the Columbus Circle entrance before the tree canopy was fully grown. The other is the result of the only straight lines in the interior of the park, extending north on the axis of what the plan labeled the Promenade (now called the Mall). Even in a cursory glance at the plan, the four lines of twenty-nine large elm trees that constitute the Promenade leap out in prominence. This is the place where Olmsted employed geometry to affirm the gregariousness of human nature. He believed that it was important for citizens to look into each other's faces, which was more likely to occur when they walked in a straight line rather than on a curving path.

The elms on the Central Park Mall in 1910

↑ Central Park Mall in winter with aged elms and two small replacements in the foreground. Note the differing branching structures of similar-aged trees.

Most of the elms on the Mall and along Fifth Avenue were replanted in 1920. Four decades later, the architectural space of the Mall would have paralleled a Gothic cathedral, with trunks forming the arcade between the nave and the side aisles, arching high to form a ceiling of filtered light. Every forty feet the stroller would cross a threshold of four trees. For visitors looking ahead, the lines of trunks marking perspective distance would have appeared as nearly solid walls. A long slice of the sky above would have formed a line drawn to infinity.

The grove is now considerably aged. The majority of trees is quite old; others are middle-aged. But there are a few random, individual replacements that are very young and, because of their youth and the fact that they are a different species, appear out of place. Both their form and size are completely unlike the older generations, and they even vary considerably in form from one to another. The spatial architecture of Olmsted's Mall is lost to these individual replacements. The intentional rhythms of the large elm trunks and the contrast of this geometry to the rest of the park are felt only peripherally, as the Mall grove now mostly blends into adjacent trees.

↑ Central Park Mall in summer with small replacements leafed out on the right.

Devising a replacement strategy for the Mall grove has become exceedingly difficult. Central Park is loved and branded. Once planted so extensively, the American elm has disappeared, due to Dutch elm disease, making the elms that remain on the Mall even more cherished. The Central Park Conservancy and the City of New York Parks Department have replaced some individual trees, though there seems to be little enthusiasm even for this approach, based on the numerous gaps in the structure where trees have not been replaced. In fact, these gaps seem more respectful of Olmsted's plan and more evocative of loss than the habit of planting random and differing "replacement" trees. In the next decade or so, however, the openings will reach a volume that will so degrade the geometry as to make a replacement strategy a necessity. Replacement could occur in entirety, in sections, or a new structure could be devised that would be respectful of Olmsted's expression but at the same time acknowledge the very different conditions the park faces today.

1945 — HERNING, DENMARK

Musical Garden

C. Th. Sørensen

TREE LIST

Carpinus betulus
European Hornbeam

As much as Olmsted admired and later stylized the agricultural landscapes of the locales he visited, Carl Theodor Sørensen (1893–1979) transformed elements of the Danish agricultural landscape—the woodland edge, the open field, the hedge, and the grove—into works of art that are both social and spatial. The Musical Garden—playful bosques of hornbeam trees pleached into hedges of clean geometrical figures—is pure sculpture. It is the design that Sørensen himself regarded as his best work and "something that gives the mind inexplicable joy."[1] What is not immediately evident in this project is the earthy and temporal knowledge of the forest that the landscape architect brought to his clear, modernist works. The campus at Århus University, which he planted from acorns, and Højstrup Park, where he devised a decades-long strategy to grow an old oak forest from eight hundred seedlings, better illustrate this.

Sørensen's 1931 master plan for Århus University proposed shaded groves of oaks on hillsides above an open stream running through the campus. When the Depression forced an unusually limited budget, the landscape architect suggested planting the area the way nature does: with acorns. The slow cultivation would trace time ever more thoughtfully, yet bear groves gracefully. The oak, native in Denmark at least since the Bronze Age, symbolically represented the region's ancient past, while the acorn looked to the future. Small round beds were laid out, with five to ten acorns planted in each, with subsequent thinning and maintenance of the saplings and trees. Today the oak groves predominate on the campus, with the expressive character that Sørensen believed was most readily attained when a plantation consisted of a single species.

↓ Giant oaks grown from acorns, planted at Århus University during the 1930s, now dominate the spatial structure of the campus.

Højstrup Park in Odense is the center of a public housing project built in 1948. Here Sørensen pushed the four-story buildings to the perimeter to frame a large courtyard park where he planted eight hundred oak seedlings. In his studies, he had observed how difficult it is for trees to thrive if they are planted individually, when they have to compete with greedy grasses or defend themselves against lawn mowers and, in housing projects, against children. He understood a principle of the forest: freestanding trees often do not grow old. Sørensen therefore consolidated the seedlings into thirty-two round beds with twenty-five seedlings forming each oak thicket, organized into eight rows of four circular beds. In the first year after the planting, the density of the round thickets was already great enough for children to hide between them. Some years later, the thickets had become thirty-two distinct groves. Residents could wander within the small, clearly formed, pyramidal oak trees, each grove thinned from natural loss. For about three decades, each copse remained distinct, but by 1991, the individual groves had become one large continuous oak forest. The designer's strategy mimicked the natural growth that occurs within a forest, while it has maintained a constant spatial volume throughout the dynamic life of this project.

Sørensen's Musical Garden was originally proposed in 1945 for a park in Horsens, but its concept was deemed too unconventional by the town council, which preferred a different design by him.

↓ Thinned, but still youthful groves of oaks at Højstrup Park

↑ The planted forest in the park at the art museum has two openings—the elliptical space of the Musical Garden and the large circular sculpture park next to the round factory.

A 1954 watercolor drawing of the project, then referred to as the Geometrical Gardens, is composed of nine figures: a circle, an oval, a square, a triangle, a pentagon, a hexagon, a heptagon, an octagon, and a thirty-three-foot straight segment, whose length is repeated in the sides of the polygons. In 1956, when the industrialist and arts patron Aage Damgaard commissioned Sørensen to incorporate garden art at his shirt factory in Herning, a small-scale version of the design was constructed there. The small rooms of the geometric figures accommodated Damgaard's sculpture collection, and a water basin was built in the circular figure as illustrated in Sørensen's drawing. Within a few years, however, the factory and the sculpture collection needed more space and moved to another site in Herning.

↓ This 1954 drawing of the Musical Garden illustrates Sørensen's initial conception for the park in Horsens.

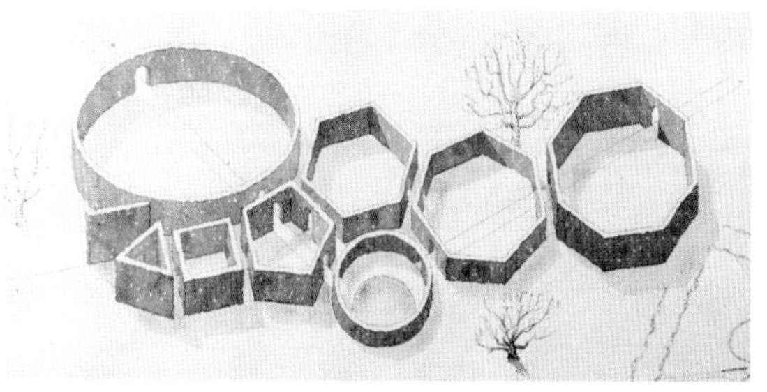

From a shared respect for art as a radical social force, Sørensen and Damgaard developed a long and trusting relationship that led Sørensen to design the master plan for the new site, the round factory, and a circular sculpture garden. Sørensen's admiration for the geometric precision of the great circular landforms the Vikings created in Denmark a thousand years earlier inspired his projects at both sites. The new factory had an enamel-painted circular courtyard that was entered via a narrow passage

↑ View of the precisely pruned exterior of hornbeam trees in a closely mown space, surrounded by a flowering meadow

↗ A framework provides precision for pruning and to openings in the figures.

from a grove of poplars. East of the round factory, a dense plantation of oak trees forms the circular sculpture garden. Nearly six hundred feet in diameter, the round clearing is a sculpture itself. A raised terrace runs along the interior edge of the woods, on which hawthorn hedges, in radial lines, create thirty-nine niches for Damgaard's collection. They face the enormous circular space and stand silhouetted against the planted oak forest. It was Sørensen's idea to graze cattle in the clearing, and for some years a herd of Herefords grazed back and forth across the plane, a moving element in a tight composition. Now it is filled with sky.

The landscape architect dedicated his last twenty years to the transformation of this rather remote site into a place where the visual arts were integrated into the everyday life of the factory. In 1983, four years after Sørensen's death, as a commemoration of the fiftieth anniversary of the Association of Danish Landscape Architects, the organization decided to plant the Musical Garden in Herning for the first time at the scale that Sørensen had proposed decades earlier.

The nine geometrical forms of the garden are placed in an elliptical opening of forest as wide as the clearing for the adjacent sculpture garden. Being able to see and walk around these geometric rooms from the outside, yet within the space of the ellipse, is a very different experience than one would have in any historic garden room and a much more sculptural expression. This is garden architecture free of buildings. The interiors and space immediately outside the "rooms" is mown, and a meadow fills the area to the planted forest edge. The rougher surfaces of the forest and meadow contrast with the precise shapes of the vegetal sculpture.

↗ The oval hedge that frames the sky is felt again in shadow.

The geometrical rooms are separated from each other by a ten-foot space that is just wide enough for sunlight to reach the full length of the hedges. In the interstitial spaces, the discovery of tight zig-zagging corridors contrasts with the openness of the hedged rooms and meadow. The locations of openings within each room are based on a V-shaped path that travels straight through the oval and pentagon to the circle and then turns to pass through the heptagon and octagon. The straight segment acts as an entrance gate to another path leading to the triangle and square. The rigorous interior spaces are filled with sky.

Planting of the hornbeam hedges began in 1983. The slow to medium growth rate of hornbeam trees, planted closer than a foot apart; their preference for sun; and their tolerance for light, shade, heavy pruning, and many soil conditions make them ideal for hedges. Sørensen had specified pruning the hedges to different heights, though not higher than twenty-six feet. The varied scale of the geometrical rooms and the range of their spatial qualities are a spectacle of whimsy and intention.

The Musical Garden is now more than twenty years old, fully grown but still quite young. The round factory has become the Carl-Henning Pedersen and Else Alfelt Museum, and the entire complex is now an international center for contemporary art. In 2009 the Herning Museum of Contemporary Art opened its doors in a new building designed by architect Steven Holl directly across from the round factory. Sørensen's park continues to give pleasure to visitors of the complex, without regard to any practical purpose, just like music, the inspiration for its name.

The structure of the hornbeam trees, exposed in winter, draws a finely detailed outline of the geometric figures.

The spatial art of the Musical Garden can be felt from within the large oval hornbeam hedge, looking through openings that lead through a taller pentagon-hedged space and beyond into a circular room.

1948 — ST. LOUIS, MISSOURI

Gateway Memorial Park

Daniel Urban Kiley

TREE LIST
KILEY'S 1964 PLAN

CANOPY TREES

Celtis occidentalis
Hackberry

Ginkgo biloba
Maidenhair Tree

Liriodendron tulipifera
Tulip Tree

Magnolia × soulangiana
Saucer Magnolia

Magnolia stellata
Star Magnolia

Quercus alba
White Oak

Quercus rubra
Red Oak

Sophora japonica
Japanese Pagodatree

Taxodium distichum
Bald Cypress

Tsuga canadensis
Canada Hemlock

FLOWERING TREES

Cercis canadensis
Eastern Redbud

Cornus florida
Flowering Dogwood

Cornus mas
Corneliancherry Dogwood

Crataegus phaenopyrum
Washington Hawthorne

Malus × arnoldiana
Arnold Crabapple

Malus sargentii
Sargent Crabapple

Prunus serrulata
Oriental Cherry

Daniel Urban Kiley (1912–2004) built a body of work that reinterprets the classical structure of trees through concepts of modern space and movement. Based on his discerning understanding of a tree's habit—the changing outline of its form as it grows, its texture, the coarseness and density of its foliage—Kiley employed various spacing schemes for the massing of particular species to draw attention to a tree's character. These sculptural masses then perform spatial functions within his landscapes, such as compression and expansion, that orchestrate movement. In a discussion of his work at the Gateway Memorial Park, in St. Louis, with Gregg Bleam in 1995, Kiley acknowledged the difficulty of specifying spatial qualities in the landscape:

> Most people are not excited about the dimensions of space. The different dimensions and what they do and how they affect, when you pick trees and place them so many feet on center, this is very important, whether they're ten feet, twelve feet, fifteen feet, or eighteen feet on center. Just like the windows in the Palazzo Farnese. Those things are what make it wonderful or not, the spatial proportion.[1]

Kiley's understanding of the effect of a landscape's spatial qualities on people, as well as his appreciation of a tree's habit, enabled him to design timeless places. Beginning with the Gateway Memorial Park at the Jefferson National Expansion Memorial, he brought the modern bosque to life in the United States.

The Gateway Arch reflects St. Louis's historical role in the expansion of the United States to the West. From a French fur-trading post established in 1764 along the Mississippi River, St. Louis soon grew into a thriving town. But it was Thomas Jefferson's negotiation of the Louisiana Purchase in 1803 and authorization of the Lewis and Clark Expedition that promoted westward expansion. St. Louis ultimately became the nation's second largest rail terminal, with warehouses, elevated rail lines, and steamboats cramming the riverfront. Plans for revitalization that coalesced in 1933 led to the acquisition of riverfront land for a national memorial. In 1947 the Gateway Memorial Park was the first major design competition after World War II, although the main structures and plantings of the winning submission by architect Eero Saarinen and Kiley were not completed until 1986.[2]

Saarinen and Kiley had served together in the Army Corps of Engineers. The war had also given Kiley his first opportunity to visit Europe, where he saw the gardens of Versailles and other classic landscapes by Le Nôtre. When Eero and sculptor Lily Saarinen first met with Kiley to work on their submission for the competition, they already had the basic concept for the arch. The stage one submission, as well as the final winning entry, illustrated the Gateway Arch much in the form it was later built—a monumental catenary arch standing in the open by the river—but the landscape would change dramatically both in conception and final built form.

↑ The 1948 competition perspective for the Gateway Memorial Park depicts a monumental catenary arch standing in the open by the river against a forested "wilderness."

← An allée of Rosehill White Ash trees today leads to the Jefferson National Expansion Memorial and Gateway Park in St. Louis.

The stage two competition perspective of the site shows the arch against a forested "wilderness" where the railroad yard existed (see above). The trees are massed together within the area, shown middle-aged and closely but irregularly spaced. The simplicity of Kiley's conceptual forest had the earthy potency essential for the soaring arch. Kiley didn't think he was making a restored forest, however. Pointing to a native wooded landscape, he is known for having said, "How could anyone be so arrogant as to try to make that! I could never do that, so I don't even try. Instead, I use geometry."[3]

A lack of funding and the Korean War interrupted Kiley's deeper involvement with the project until 1957. During this interval, he developed his own practice, and between 1952 and 1954 proposed garden plans for nearly one hundred residential plots in Hollin Hills, Virginia. In 1955 he created his most celebrated work, the Miller Garden, in collaboration with Saarinen, in Columbus, Indiana. Here Kiley's free plan of trees and hedges was largely based on a ten-foot grid, though, in situations overwhelmed with geometry, he energized space with groves outside the grid. Eight distinct tree gardens structure the spatial movement of the site, each of a particular species and regular spacing. One of the most inventive is the rotated allée of honey locusts—planted fourteen feet on center—that create a loggia through which a sweeping view of the garden's open meadow can be seen. Each of the landscape's intimate and private groves swirls around the Miller House with a rare spatial complexity.

Kiley's intervening work profoundly affected his design of the Gateway Memorial Park landscape. In addition, the problem of how to maintain rail service had forced a comprehensive reassessment of the whole site plan. In a number of studies, plan and section took on various curves that reflected the arch, while the railroad appeared in both open cuts and tunnels, its final location raising the base of the arch. In 1993 Kiley recalled his approach to the landscape for the memorial:

> Well, one of the big things I was trying to tell Eero during the designing phases, both in the first and second phases, I was trying to interject a more spatial mystery to the whole site.... And that the landscape should relate more spatially, visually/spatially, like a walk in nature. It should be like a walk in the woods, and you don't know what's next. And it's leading you, always leading you. And sort of—I call it spatial continuity. And, Eero would say, well, draw it.[4]

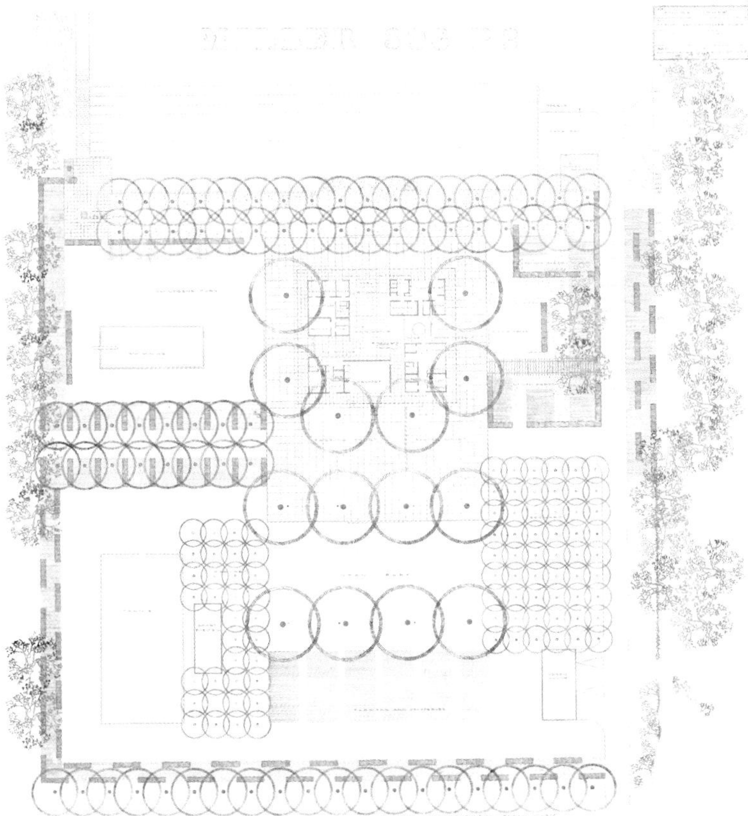

→ This 1955 plan of the Miller Garden illustrates several tree gardens of different species and spacing.

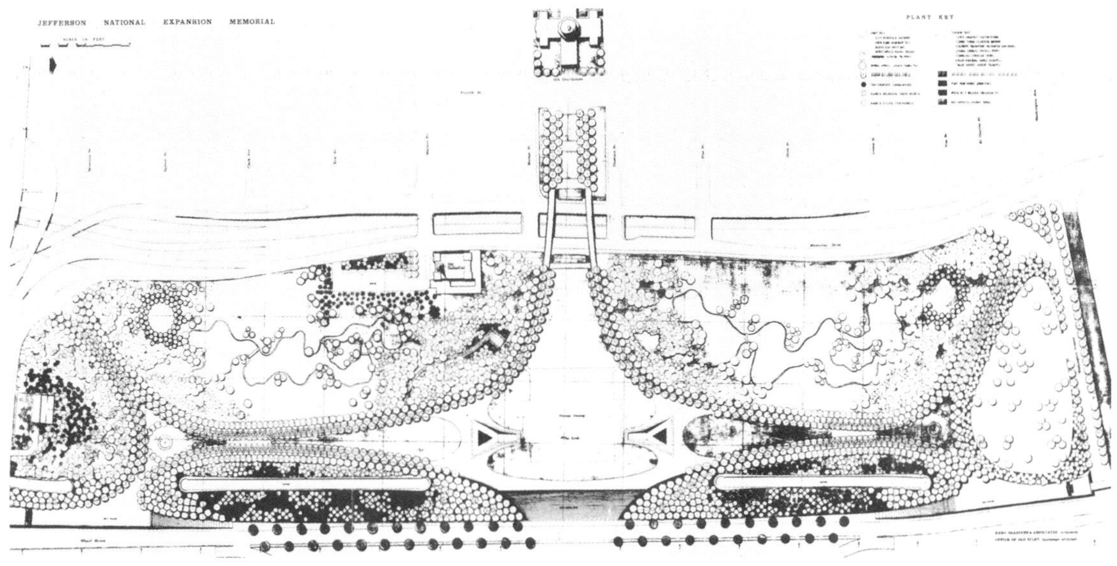

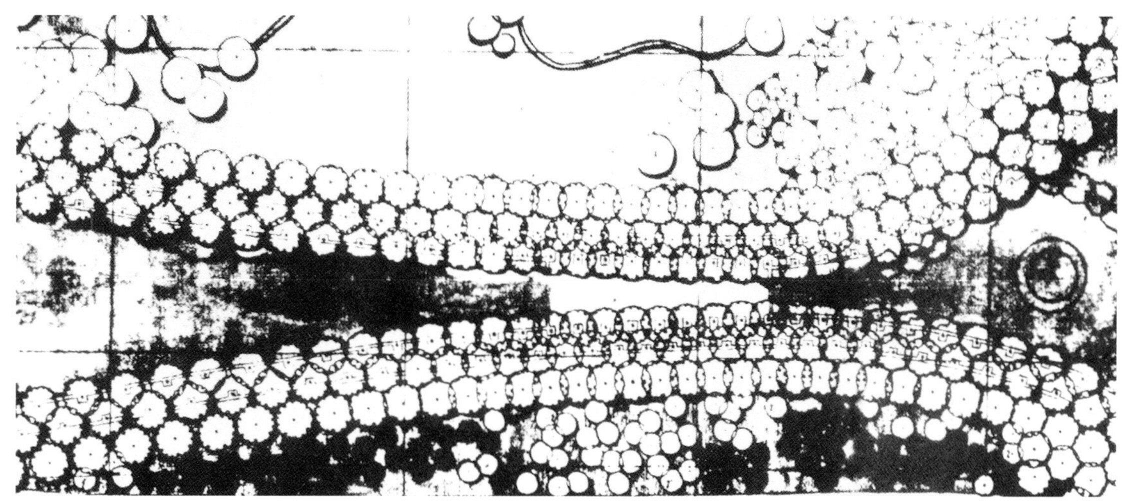

The 1964 plan for the Gateway Memorial Park proposed a tall forest of Tulip Poplar allées, and a densely planted, mixed woodland contrasting with open meadows.

Kiley's strategic spatial continuity is exemplified by six lines of closely spaced tulip poplars and an intimate corridor of space that merges and opens twice before reaching the arch.

As Kiley was refining the site design after 1957, he reassessed the extensive, tall tree forest originally proposed for the whole site. By concentrating this forest along the walkways leading to the arch and the courthouse, he achieved his most strategic "sense of movement of spatial continuity."[5] Six lines of closely spaced tulip trees create an intimate corridor that contrasts to the monumental open space surrounding the arch. The lines also expand and contract as they lead toward it: from the corner entrances to the site, the lines separate before merging into one mass, opening again on alignment with the arch, before narrowing and opening again at the arch itself. A visitor moving through the trees can see all six lines of tree trunks in straight, curving, and radiating diagonal lines.

↑ In this 1962 rendering, Kiley shows the approach to the Gateway Arch from the south in the winter.

↓ In a 1963 design development drawing, Kiley depicts six lines of tulip poplars capable of expanding as necessary to follow the curves of the walks while the trunks could be seen in straight, curving, and radiating diagonal lines.

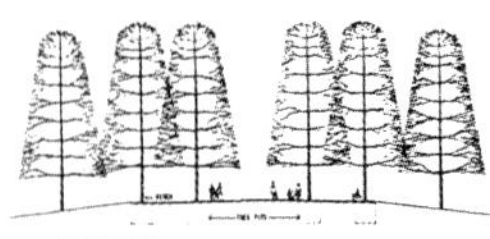

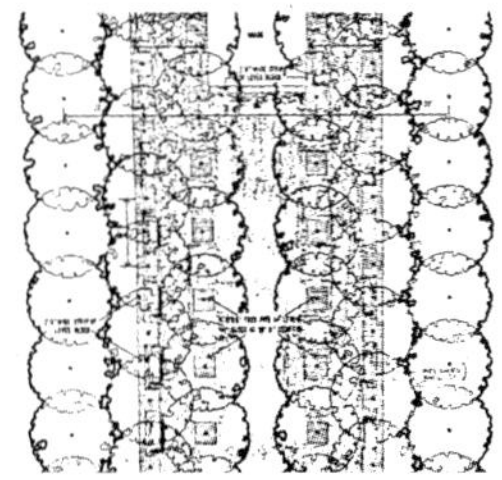

Kiley was familiar with the beautiful tulip trees he'd seen in the forests of Virginia, where the closely growing trees might lose their branches for three-quarters of their height while maintaining a conical crown at the top. He selected the species because of its tall stature, growing three times as tall as it is wide, and because it grows fast. It could soar up, cathedral-like, to a landscape scale proportional with the soaring arch. In a design development drawing from 1962, Kiley illustrated a straight segment of the rhythmically ordered forest of tulip poplars in an approach to the Gateway Arch from the south in the winter. The drawn perfection of this vertical enclosure of trees, their marching geometry, and the distant presence of the Gateway Arch would benefit in reality from natural processes that would individuate the character of each tree.

Kiley knew the spacing of Le Nôtre's Tuileries in Paris, where the trees are twelve feet and six inches on center.[6] Some of his original concept drawings for the memorial reflected this spacing, but this was deemed too close by the National Park Service (NPS) to be approved.

In his final conceptual planting plan of 1964, Kiley also proposed two circles of bald cypresses, northwest and southeast of the ponds. Naturally found in pure stands near swamps, these stately, textured groves frame views of the ponds and the distant Gateway Arch. Bald

cypresses are deciduous conifers and columnar, particularly when young. They may grow to one hundred feet tall and one-third as wide, becoming more irregular in old age. Kiley's proposed bald cypress circles were densely planted in 1980, and they form spectacular enclosures today. Additionally, there are small groves of bald cypresses set into the ponds, and others located adjacent to the grand staircase.

In the remainder of the site, Kiley contrasts the qualities of irregular, densely planted forest with low open meadow. The only spots where trees appear in smaller groups (but almost never singly) are tucked into the curving recesses of the ponds or occasionally in the parking lot. Descending from the tall forest of the tulip tree allées is a densely planted, mixed wood of white and red oaks, hackberry, ginkgo, and flowering trees at the edges that clearly distinguish the forest from the two large open meadows.

By the end of 1963, stainless steel sections of the arch had reached higher than one hundred feet but the landscape was bare. Kiley's involvement with the project ceased after his completion of the 1964 design development drawings. The landscape program suffered from cost reductions; ponds appeared, disappeared, and reappeared; and the director of the NPS questioned the extensive use of underbrush because of policing problems, as well as the quantity and species of trees. The NPS subsequently revised the plant list and replaced the majestic tulip tree with the Rosehill White Ash, *Fraxinus americana* 'Rosehill.' Consideration was given to growth factors, such as soils, light, and the urban tolerance of the Rosehill ash, but none was given to the habit of the tulip tree that Kiley had specified.

↓ View of an allée of ash as it curves into the distance

Rosehill ashes were first planted in 1972 at the spacing approved in Kiley's 1964 plan. The planting was completed by 1986. From 1981 until 2004, dead ash trees were replaced in kind, with the dead trees being removed and replaced by young trees of the same species. By 2009, 150 missing ash trees out of 900 in the allées had not been replaced, due to the threat of the emerald ash borer. While two substantial Cultural Landscape Reports, from 1996 and 2010, provide a thorough history of the process, they do not address the hard questions that will determine the future of the allées: Does in-kind replacement slowly degrade the structure of the allées over time as they become a collection of trees of different sizes? With the directive for no further replacements, could the increasing holes in the mass provide the opportunity for a replacement strategy that has a

↑↑ Problems with disease and replacements are evident in the ash allées.

↑ Six lines of 'Rosehill' ash at their closest spacing. Note recent replacements.

structural component rather than addresses individual trees? In a conversation with Bleam in 1996, Kiley suggested "a rhythmic replacement program," a strategy that would be delightful and satisfy the need for replacement without doing so in a spotty manner.[7] Finally, if the Rosehill ash is no longer being planted, should a structural replacement strategy recall the tulip poplars and/or address the idea of structural diversity?

Other changes to Kiley's 1964 plan include the quantity of trees and species specified for the site. The NPS planting plans have doubled the number of tree species even while they eliminated half of the species that Kiley had proposed. In addition, they reduced the overall quantity of trees by nearly half, thus altering the configuration of trees on the site in general. During Kiley's involvement, the landscape generally changed from the concept of the symbolic forested wilderness to the final design of tall tree allées, forest, and meadow. Since the NPS took over the planting plans, the contrast of forest and meadow has been obscured by the conventional park paradigm: randomly planted trees and manicured lawns.

Many questions about the future of the site may be answered by Michael Van Valkenburgh Associates (MVVA), the landscape architects that won a 2009 competition, The City+The Arch+The River, to create an iconic setting for the Gateway Arch by honoring its immediate surroundings and weaving connections and transitions from the city and the arch grounds to the Mississippi River. MVVA's master plan doubles the size of the site by expanding it across the river to include its east bank in Illinois, where the East Wetland Preserve uses stormwater gathered from East St. Louis to create sixty acres of new wildlife habitat. A system of canopy trails elevates visitors above the Mississippi flood berm, allowing them to appreciate the boundless horizon of the American Midwest. This restoration and expansion of the memorial will be constructed by October 28, 2015, the fiftieth anniversary of the completion of the arch.

→ The MVVA master plan expands across the river to create sixty acres of new wildlife habitat and a system of elevated canopy trails.

CASINO QUEEN
CARGILL SILOS
EADS BRIDGE
POPLAR STREET BRIDGE
LACLEDE'S LANDING
CHOUTEAU'S LANDING
I-70
BUSCH STADIUM

1963 — BOSTON, MASSACHUSETTS

Linden Quincunx, Christian Science Plaza

Sasaki Associates

TREE LIST

Tilia cordata
Littleleaf Linden

Not a single tree has been lost from the nearly two hundred that shape the Linden Quincunx at Boston's Christian Science Plaza. This success is largely due to the selection and care of the trees before they were installed and the innovative design detailing of the underground environment in which they grow. A rare and early example of modern design in urban redevelopment, the unusual quincunx has grown in stature over the decades, so its care has been recently recalibrated to adjust to its mature size and density.

The Mother Church, the world headquarters for the Church of Christ, Scientist, which gives the plaza its name, was built in 1894 amid a tightly packed network of streets and four-story row houses in old Boston, an area that survived until the 1960s, when thirty acres surrounding it were cleared for redevelopment. In 1963 Araldo Cossutta, one of four principals in the firm of I. M. Pei and who had earlier worked for Le Corbusier, became the head of the plaza's design team, which also included Stuart Dawson of the multidisciplinary firm Sasaki Associates in Watertown, Massachusetts. Together they created a piazza in modern form, described at the time as lean and muscular. The simple and monumental pool, grove, and fountain distill and magnify encounters with processes of nature: wind and reflection, bright sun and deep shade, rainbows seen through sparkling drops of water.

Beloved for four decades, the tightly planted Linden Quincunx at the Christian Science Plaza for which Sasaki Associates won an Honor Award from the American Society of Landscape Architects (ASLA), gives form to the monumental square, separating it from the street while providing a contrasting experience of intimacy for the pedestrian. A single line of trees begins in the tight space between

↓ An aerial photo from the 1970s shows the Linden Quincunx at the center spiraling on the east side of the high-rise building in the complex (casting a shadow straight north) before it travels straight west.

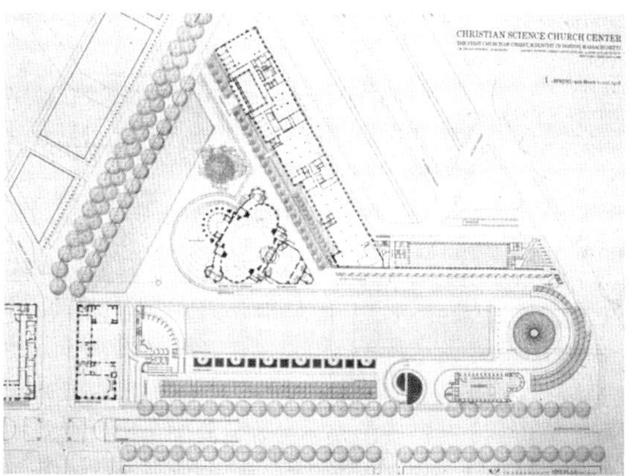

↑ Plan illustrating the single line of lindens as it spirals around the circular fountain to form the quincunx before traveling the length of the monumental pool.

↗ View of the Linden Quincunx from across the pool and perennial gardens

the fountain and the arcade building, spirals into an allée, and gathers into a quincunx (see page 23), that repeats itself many times before reaching the other side of the fountain. There the lines of trees break for the high-rise administration building and underground parking exit, before continuing in a straight quincunx running the length of the pool.

Looking at the quincunx from across the pool, the trunks appear to be staggered. The experience is quite different, however, when walking within the grove. There, one sees multiple rows of trees set in diagonals running in both directions. Walking underneath the large singular canopy feels like walking in a forested cathedral. The dramatic change in microclimate that the trees create is felt suddenly and intensely. The expansiveness of the civic space provides a strong contrast to the personal experience of walking among the trunks.

The designers at Sasaki Associates were inspired in their choice of trees by a historical garden of perennials and trees that had existed at the church on Huntington Avenue before the redevelopment started. American linden trees in that garden had been individually pruned to regularize their shapes. To provide continuity from the earlier garden to the civic plaza, Cossutta and Dawson proposed an aerial hedge of pleached Littleleaf Linden trees because linden trees are fairly slow growing and receptive to pleaching. Sasaki carefully studied the spatial dimensions between the trees in relation both to the experience of a person walking within the grove and to the volume of the collective mass as experienced architecturally on the site, taking into account its growth over time. A full-scale model, using sonotubes to approximate trunks, helped determine the spacing for the three lines of trees: twelve feet on center, which produces a diagonal spacing of fourteen feet on center.

← The quincunx pattern of the freshly planted linden trees can be seen in this aerial photo of the Christian Science Plaza taken before construction was completed in 1973. The paving and concrete planters in this view are now dominated by the mature linden grove.

According to Dawson, the success of the planting, with not a single tree lost in four decades, can be attributed to three particular efforts: the preselection of trees, the construction of continuous soil trenches, and suspended paving. When the First Church of Christ, Scientist

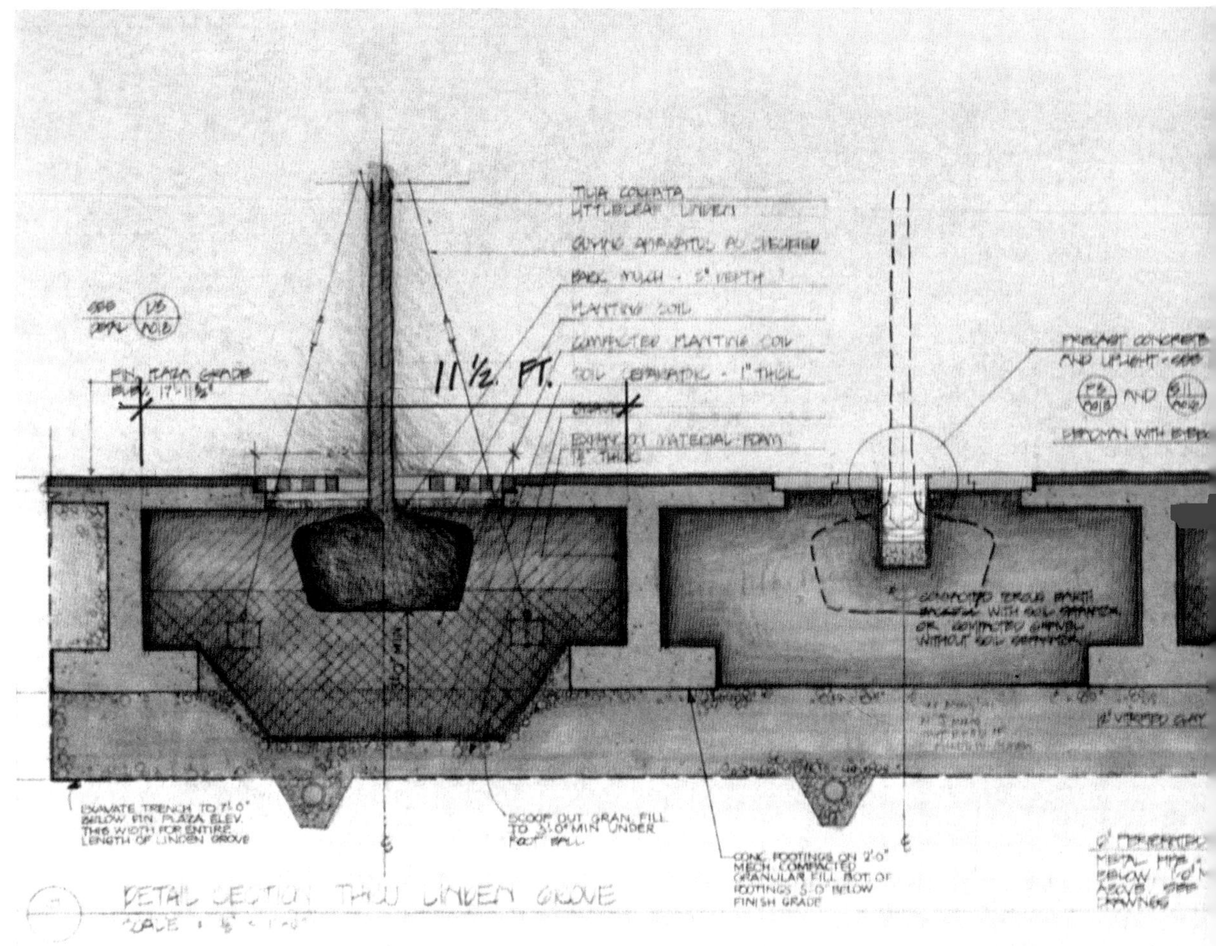

↑ A detailed section through the Linden Quincunx illustrates the infrastructure for creating continuous soil trenches and suspended paving.

approved Dawson's proposal to preselect the trees, two hundred Littleleaf Lindens of four-inch caliper were tagged in a nursery in Chicago four years before they were planted. During that time they were root-pruned and grew two more inches in caliper before being planted in Boston.

Innovative now, prescient then, three continuous soil trenches running the length of the Linden Quincunx were installed, allowing the lindens to grow into large, healthy shade trees. After all, the site was being redeveloped from the demolition of densely built structures, and the soil conditions would have been compromised. Although there is also underground parking on the site, the grove is planted on existing subgrade excavated to a depth of seven feet below the plaza elevation. Above the subgrade is a layer of gravel within which perforated, corrugated metal pipes drain away excess water and upon which insulated concrete footings rest. A soil-separating membrane keeps the compacted soil, a minimum depth of three feet

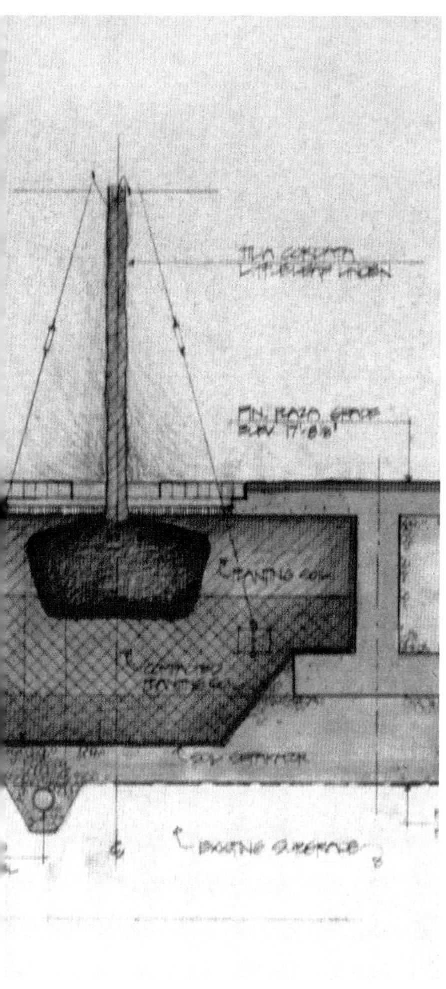

↗ In this photo from the 1980s, the crowns are raised to five feet and trimmed individually, producing separate shadows.

below the root ball, from mixing with the gravel. The planting soil is a mix of 20 percent sand and 20 percent peat with 60 percent loam. The generous width and continuous length of each trench allows air and water to nourish the roots. Absolutely integral with the soil trenches is a suspended paving system that protects the soil from compaction due to traffic from people or equipment moving around on the surface.

Littleleaf Lindens grow nearly twice as tall as wide in the open and grow even more upright when planted closely. They are tolerant of pollution and therefore widely planted in cities. They appreciate full sun, and their small, glossy green leaves turn golden yellow in the fall. Tolerant of pruning, they develop very dense branching as they age. When the lindens were first planted, their small canopies cast individual shadows on the pavement below, providing alternating bright sun and dark circular shadows to the pedestrian. Although Sasaki had proposed an aerial hedge of flat planes, while the trees' canopies were still too small to touch one another, they were pruned individually into

↑ By 1997, the Quincunx had become a collective structure but the space underneath the canopy was very confined and darkly shaded.

oval-rounded shape, a form they naturally take as they age. Eventually, when their canopies started to touch, they grew into a singular mass, but shearing with an aerial stencil that duplicated an identical oval-rounded shape on each tree made them look like topiary. Pruning only the outer surface of the tree crowns also produced extremely dense branching on the exterior that did not allow air to flow or light to reach interior branches. The dense shadows caused some of the interior branches to begin to die.

In 2000 the First Church of Christ, Scientist commissioned landscape architecture firm Reed Hilderbrand Associates to develop a rehabilitation plan for the entire site and to design a garden on Huntington Street at the new entrance to the Mary Baker Eddy Library. The rehabilitation plan guided the transformation of the flowering beds in the planters along the pool from annuals to the largest perennial garden in Boston. The plan also included a maintenance strategy for the Linden Quincunx. By this time, the space underneath the canopy was darkly shaded and nearly oppressive. Reed Hilderbrand Associates proposed raising the crowns by pruning the lower limbs. The space underneath the canopy was thus elevated from five to eight feet to extend vision and movement. The firm also recommended crown thinning—the selective removal of interior branches to increase light penetration and air movement throughout the crowns of the trees. This method of hand pruning produces a looser outline of each tree

↓ View of the perennial garden between the pool and the Linden Quincunx

↑ Today the Quincunx is more than four decades old, without the loss of a single tree. The crowns have been raised to eight feet and thinned to increase light penetration, producing a looser outline of each tree that emphasizes the collective mass.

while still emphasizing the collective mass. As a consequence of these changes, the interior of the canopy receives more light and is filling in more evenly. The overall form is looser and the trees are healthier.

From a distance, each of the trees appears distinct, yet they also form a beautiful collective structure, largely due to the fact that there have never been replacements. A closer look reveals the individuality of each tree as it has aged differently. Bending slightly one direction or another, some have larger bodies than others, and the marks left from former branches vary. Their fall color also varies slightly from one to the next. The Linden Quincunx remains a rare example of an American public space where, for four decades, the power of a single species that is tightly spaced has enlivened an extraordinary landscape design and created contrasting experiences of intimate and monumental space, bright sun and deep shade.

1995 — LONDON, ENGLAND

Tate Modern

Kienast Vogt Partner

TREE LIST

BIRCH TREES

Betula jacquemontii
Whitebarked Himalayan Birch

Betula maximowicziana
Monarch Birch

Betula papyrifera
Paper Birch

Betula pendula
Silver Birch

Betula platyphylla var. *'Szechuanica'*
Szechuan White Birch

CLUMPS OF TREES

Fraxinus americana
White Ash

Fraxinus augustifolia
Narrowleaf Ash

Platanus × acerifolia
London Planetree

Platanus occidentalis
American Planetree

Platanus orientalis
Oriental Planetree

MIXED HEDGE TREES

Carpinus betulus
European Hornbeam

Crataegus monogyna
Singleseed Hawthorn

Fagus sylvatica
European Beech

TALL, RECTANGULAR, PIONEERING THICKETS—freestanding bosquets crowded with slender birch trees—supply volumes of abstract forest to this recently transformed landscape. Geometry comes into play in the form of the mass rather than in the placement of trunks. Located on the Thames River in London, Bankside is one of the oldest settlements in Britain. For centuries it experienced uses hostile to the city: boisterous establishments, theaters (such as Shakespeare's Globe Theater in 1599), and, in the twentieth century, industry. After World War II, the area declined altogether until it became attractive for the city's expansion in the 1990s. Reconstruction of the Globe began in 1995, the same year that the Bankside Power Station, which had been disused since 1981, was adapted by Herzog & de Meuron into the Tate Modern art gallery. The Kienast Vogt Partner's landscape for the Tate Modern speaks to the history of this postindustrial site and the urban forest.

→ Tall rectangular thickets of slender birch trees are at the center of Kienast Vogt Partner's design for the Tate Modern in London.

↑ The birches take the form of rectangular copses, acknowledging that the trees represent the natural activity of birch trees rather than suggesting they have naturally colonized the site.

Dieter Kienast (1945–98) was already a renowned landscape architect when he joined Günther Vogt to form Kienast Vogt Partner in 1995 (now Vogt Landscape Architects), creating a modern and independent language of design that is architecturally structured and richly attentive to natural processes. The firm calls rigid order into question, but precisely considered structure, based on local conditions, nonetheless prevails. The concept of architectural groups of pioneering birches invading and rescuing this postindustrial site in London exemplifies this independent design language.

The conversion of the Bankside Power Station building into the Tate Modern was so costly that (as predictably often happens) little of the budget was left for the landscape. Kienast Vogt Partner's response was a minimalism that is a product of that limitation but is also, more importantly, a reflection of a long-practiced and deeply held conviction that clarity communicates intensity. The singular use of birch in the thickets is evocative and spatially powerful. The concentration of birches, with some trunks only inches apart, both evokes their biological niche in the ecosystem and achieves an unusual spatial organization in which geometry informs the perimeter of the masses but not the placement of trees within.

The choice of birch trees symbolizes the transformation from abandonment to renewal. Birch is a pioneer plant that thrives on fallow land and birch woods commonly populate riverbanks. Trees of this

↑ Vogt Landscape Architects's 2009 plan for the third phase of the project illustrates the rectangular copses that pierce the lawn and paving along the river north of the Tate, while to the south the firm's design references former subterranean oil tanks with two circular sitting walls directly above them and a long, complementary curving thicket of birch trees along the walkway.

family naturally appear early when ground—whether it be postindustrial or postglacial—is available to be colonized. As a plant pollinated by wind, birches can establish themselves quickly. After the last ice age, for example, birches rapidly spread north in Europe in the wake of retreating glaciers.

Another important function that birches fulfill in ecosystems is that of improving soils. Birches are deep-rooted, and their roots draw up nutrients into their branches and leaves, which the trees use for their growth and then deposit on the surface when their leaves fall. Birch trees also tolerate the accumulation of heavy metals in their leaves, a process of soil remediation in a postindustrial landscape such as the site at the Tate Modern.

The geometric copses take the form of rectangular bands, about ten feet wide and four or five times as long, in front of the museum building. These rectangular groves achieve the spatial experience of confinement and expansiveness at the same time. Eight rectangular copses separate the pedestrian promenade along the river from the discrete spaces they create at the Bankside Gardens—the entrance plaza, the grass panel, and the east and west courts. The composition is nuanced by three pairs of rectangular thickets that slide forward and backward, defining walkways, and piercing lawn and paving. The designers have described the interlocking spaces as neither a public square nor a private garden but a hybrid English square.

Ironically, the birch thickets create a pastoral setting on the front lawn of the former power plant.

Birch thickets create a tunnel leading to the Thames River.

↑ Birch copses frame an expansive lawn from busy public paths on the Thames River.

The birch thickets are dense, planted with both multistemmed trees and single trunks that are planted so closely together that they appear to be multistemmed, in mulched and lighted beds that are flush with both the lawn and pavement. The groves are regularly maintained, with trees being thinned as frequently as necessary to accommodate new growth and preserve the volume of the thickets. Their creamy white trunks and cinnamon-colored branches brighten an industrial gray or dismal London day.

Kienast Vogt Partner has allowed a few trees to escape the rectangular copses, taking their places within the grass panel where visitors spread out in the space formed by the thickets. Thousands of yellow and white daffodils that are arranged in squares bloom on the lawn in spring. In appreciation of natural processes, the designers expect this geometry to fade in years to come. In front of the first-floor cafe, a small freestanding birch grove forms a space for outdoor seating on a stepped slope facing the Thames, where visitors can sit and converse or watch the regular spectacle of low and high tides.

Gravel is the single material used throughout the site for hard surfaces. Whether it is loose, bonded, or rolled into asphalt, the regular size of the stones suggests treatment by the power of water or industry, two generating forces at this site. The central plaza, paved by gravel rolled into asphalt, is bounded at the sides by the birch thickets and spreads out between the riverside promenade and the chimney of the former power station where it meets the turbine hall and becomes the entrance platform.

In 2009, the Tate Modern commissioned Vogt Landscape Architects to engage in the third phase of the project. A new addition by Herzog & de Meuron, scheduled to open in 2012, is being constructed southwest of the Tate, where the former power station's circular subterranean oil tanks will not only provide the physical foundation for the new building but also be accessible to visitors. Vogt Landscape Architects's plan references the tanks with a circular sitting wall directly above them at ground level on an exposed-aggregate asphalt plaza south of the Tate.

An existing grove of plane trees south of the old power plant will be incorporated into the firm's third-phase plan, in addition to proposals for nine new clusters of trees and three linear thickets that will be planted in 2015 in locations to the east, west, and south of the Tate. The linear planting proposed to the east of the Tate employs a forest succession strategy: faster-growing Silver and Paper Birch trees are proposed to overstand the hedge, creating an immediate volume, until the slower-growing beech and hornbeam trees gain a mature profile.

The new landscape design incorporates a larger number of birch species in the proposed thickets to create a richer planting palette, but will maintain the expression of geometry, though a different form, in the thickets' overall mass. Seventy percent of the trees in the new plantings will be Silver Birch, but they will be mixed with Paper, Whitebarked Himalayan, Asian Szechuan, and Monarch Birches. Complementing the existing rectangular thickets to the north, the geometry to the south takes the form of an S-curve that plays off an independently curving south entrance path. Linear timber benches follow the S-curve on alternating sides of the entrance path between the existing grove of plane trees and the dynamic new concentration of birches that engage this postindustrial landscape.

↓ Directly south of the Tate Modern, an exuberant thicket of birches will be planted in a curving retaining system, constructed of concrete and Thames Valley flint stone, a design influenced by the sedimentary deposits that can be found along the Thames River.

Some of the birches populate the grass panel, encouraging visitors to spread out among them.

1995 — MUNICH, GERMANY

Riemer Park
Latitude Nord

TREE LIST

FROM PARK MASTER PLAN

Abies alba
Silver Fir

Acer campestre
Hedge Maple

Acer platanoides
Norway Maple

Acer pseudoplatanus
Sycamore Maple

Betula pendula
European Birch

Carpinus betulus
European Hornbeam

Fagus sylvatica
European Beech

Fraxinus excelsior
European Ash

Picea abies
Norway Spruce

Pinus sylvestris
Scotch Pine

Populus tremula 'Erecta'
Upright Aspen

Prunus padus
European Birdcherry

Prunus avium
Sweet Cherry

Pyrus pyraster
Wild Pear

Quercus petraea
Sessile Oak

Quercus robur
English Oak

Salix caprea
Goat Willow

Sorbus aucuparia
European Mountainash

Sorbus torminalis
Wild Service Tree

Tilia cordata
Littleleaf Linden

Ulmus glabra
Scotch Elm

→ Extensive and precisely contoured landforms structure the ground plane of the park.

THE DESIGN ELEMENTS at Munich's Riemer Park are basic—tree masses and landforms—but the result is radically sculptural and viscerally spatial. Twenty thousand trees were planted in the transformation of a former airport into a park that is now the centerpiece of a mixed-use development. The new park celebrates, with gracious frankness, the making of a landscape. Geometry, employed as axes across the site and in gridded blocks of trees, provides spatial orientation and gregarious groves. Perspective is activated by tree masses that contain the foreground and diminish as they are layered into the distance. Tight enclosures of dark woods contrast and give form to sunny,

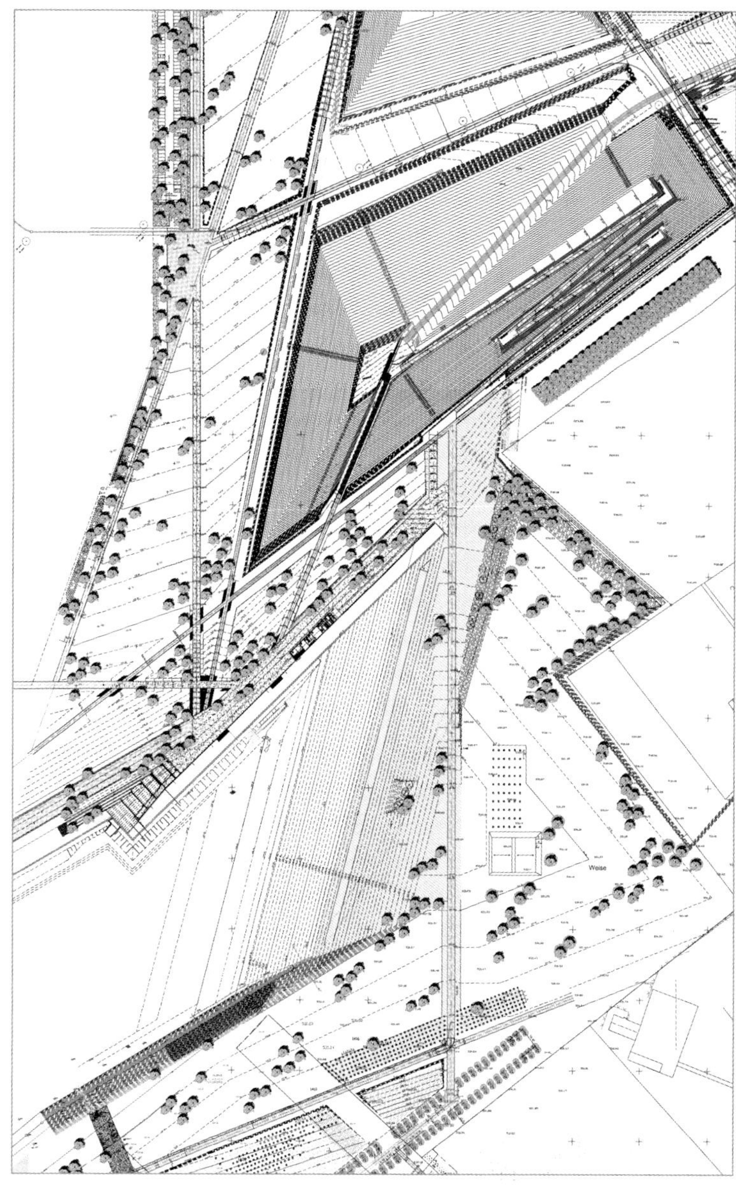

↑ A garden shed borders beds of perennials remaining from the Bundesgartenschau and a woodland plantation.

↗ Dense clumps of multi-stemmed birch trees form an entrance to the park from the town.

flowering meadows. Forests break open for pedestrian routes that slice through them, while small groves shelter people having picnics. Riemer Park is a rich and varied experience that, twenty or fifty years from now, will have an amplified structure and complexity, making it one of the most stunning designed landscapes anywhere.

The design of the park, which received the first International Urban Landscape Award in 2006, is the work of Gilles Vexlard and Laurence Vacherot of Latitude Nord, Paris, the product of a winning competition entry in 1995. It opened in 2006 on the exposed plain east of Munich, a site that functioned as the city's major airport from the end of World War II until 1992. As is frequently the case in Europe, a temporary garden exhibition (Bundesgartenschau) was held in the park in 2005, introducing thousands of people to the area and its opportunities for dwelling and commerce. After the fair ended, the site was transformed into a public park. To the north of Riemer Park is a new development of business parks, housing for sixteen thousand people, stores, restaurants, and exhibition halls. To the south are farms, woodland, gravel works, and low-density housing.

The U-shaped site surrounds the new town north of it, so it is convenient to walk or bike into the park from schools, stores, and residential areas, which have their own small parks and playgrounds. The size of Riemer Park is an exceptional 815 acres, nearly the size of Central Park. The northern part adjacent to the town is the most structured and active. A skateboard park, basketball courts, Ping-Pong tables, and playfields facilitate specific sports. Perennial gardens that remain from the Bundesgartenschau are north of the spine, a six-hundred-foot terrace that runs one and a half miles from the west to a swimming lake in the east. To the south, large meadows flow through masses of trees. Straight paths cut through these groves and large open meadows where jogging, biking, and walking predominate.

↖ Picnicking within lines of shade in a bosquet

← A bosquet in the late afternoon surrounded by a meadow and a distant pine plantation

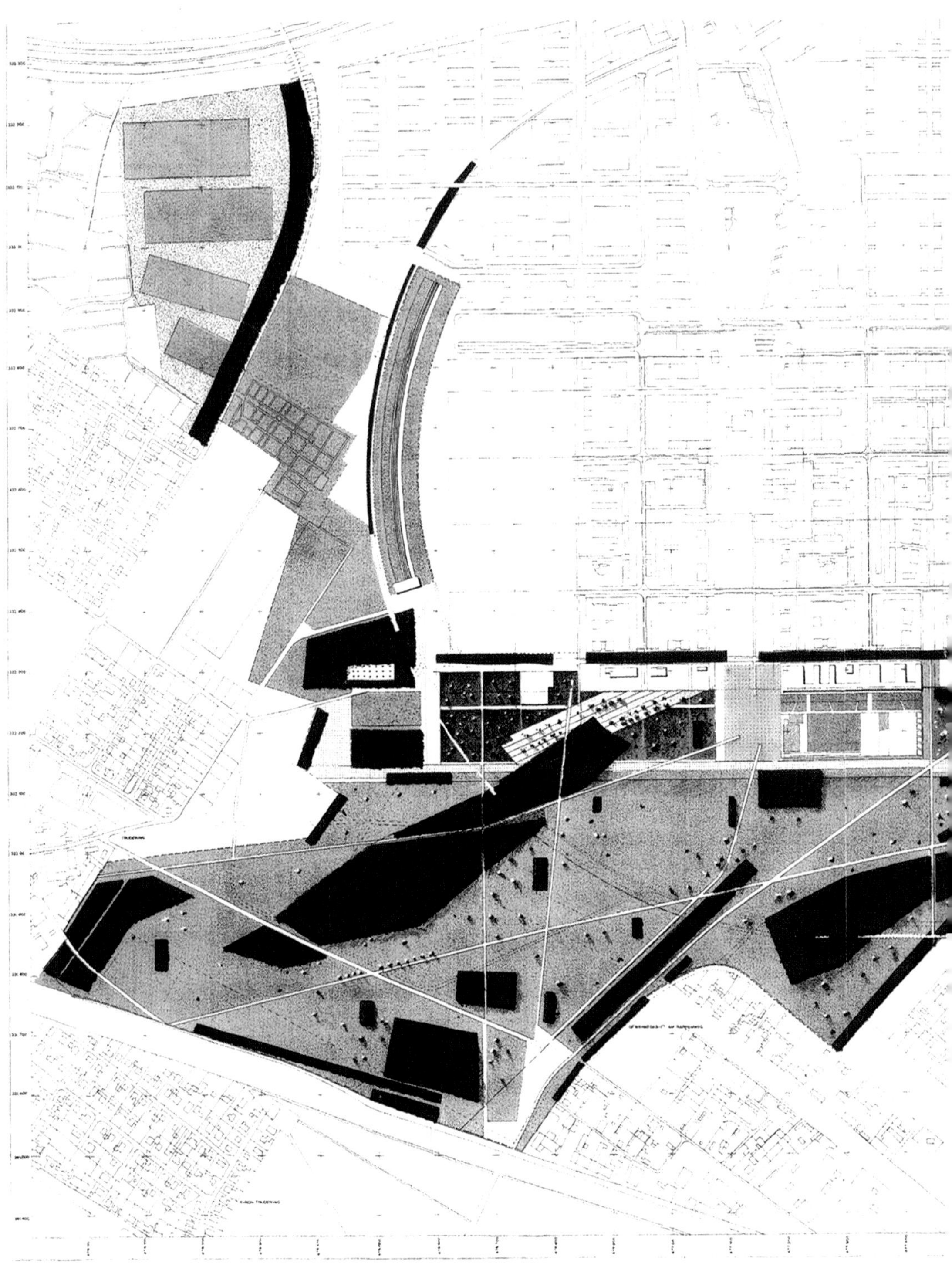

The U-shaped park surrounds the new town to the north in this plan by Latitude Nord. Woodlands and the lake follow the diagonal lines of the region's geography.

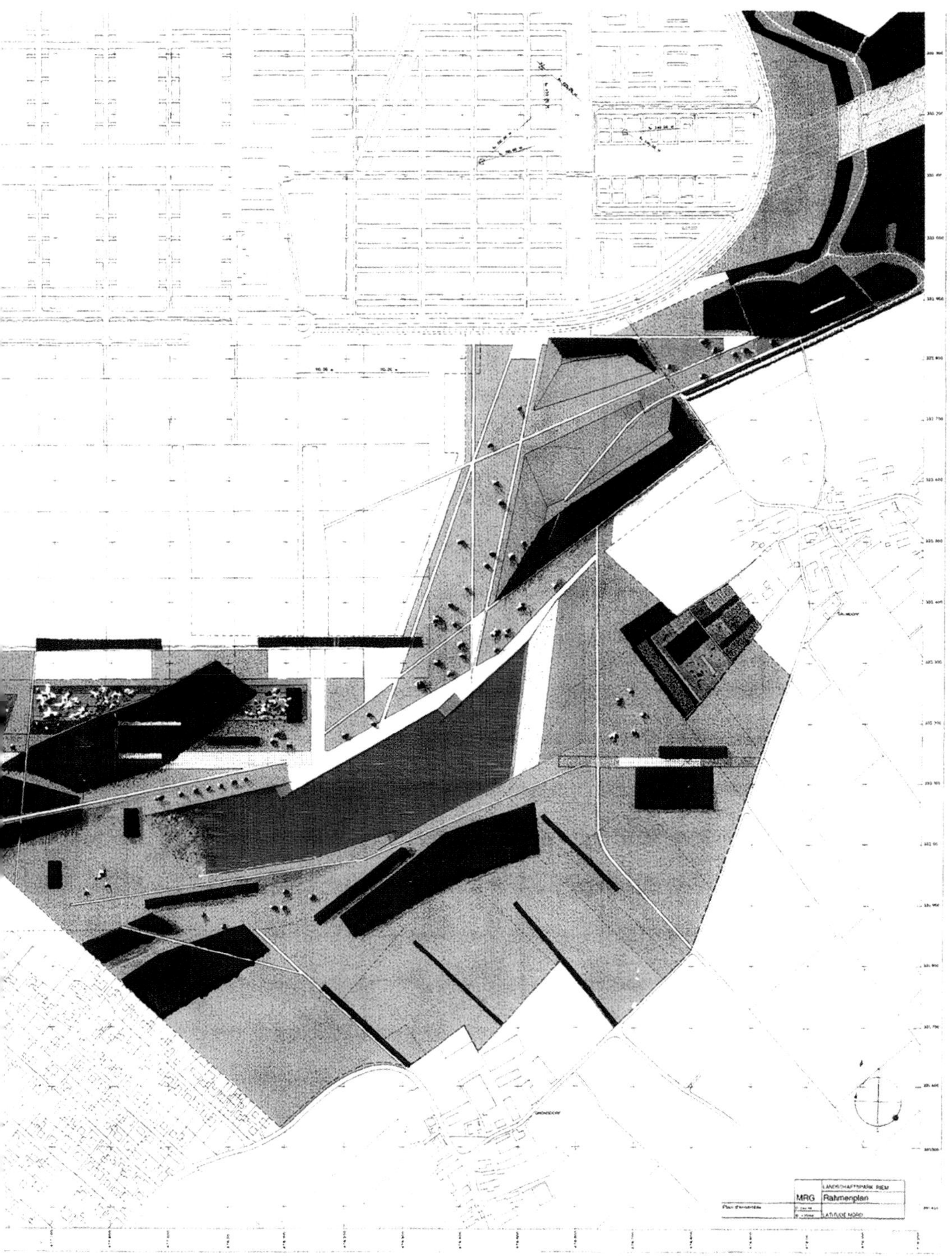

In the center, running east/west, is the raised pedestrian spine that separates intimate gardens and sports facilities from meadows and groves to the south. Small rectangular bosquets dot the meadows.

↑ The geology and woodland composition of the region runs diagonally from the northeast to the southwest. Vernacular field patterns and even the primary runway of the former airport on the site (the oval with a diagonal line on the drawing) followed this orientation.

The diagonal orientation of the woodland plantations and swimming lake is derived from an analysis that combined regional physical geography and cultural history. By looking at maps of the hydrology and woodland composition of the region, the landscape architects discovered that the largest blocks of existing woodland, as well as the River Isar, which runs through the center of Munich and the Englischer Garten, the city's main park, are both oriented diagonally from the northeast to the southwest. The organization of vernacular field patterns and pathways that overlaid this geography left a similar diagonal imprint on the land before the airport was built. Even the primary runway of the former airport followed this direction. The structural woodland plantations proposed by Latitude Nord that follow the northeast/southwest diagonal, in multiple overlaid orders, thus reflect a former cultural pattern that itself expressed the underlying physical region.

The strategy for planting the park's twenty thousand trees is based on principles of spacing that emphasize the idea that this is a constructed landscape made for human perception. Geometric masses of trees form large woodland plantations, wooded bands, bosquets, and groups of individual trees. There is no pretense here that these trees regenerated on their own nor that natural processes are not integral to their growth. This is a planted forest, and the organization of trees provides a structure for spatial and geometric innovation.

The woodland plantations are massive. Thousands of tightly planted trees create immense volumes that carve out vast meadows. All of the trees are planted in a grid ten feet on center, but the diversity of species and textures is wide-ranging. The existing forests in the region of Munich are predominately pine, oak, and hornbeam. Linden, Norway maple, Sycamore maple, ash, sweet cherry, and birch can also be found. The bold, large-scale plantations at Riemer Park are predominantly pine and oak, but the tree list for the park includes the above forest species as well as silver fir, hedge maple, beech, spruce, aspen, bird cherry, wild pear, sessile oak, goat willow, mountain ash, wild service tree, and scotch elm.

The blocks of pine and oak within the plantations are still very young, and their character will change dramatically as they age. Today it is still difficult to walk within the oaks, because their canopies are so low to the ground. The even-aged pines will grow quickly to compete for light. Pine branches fill the space from the ground up and from one trunk to the next. But pines, in particular, lose their needles and lower branches as they age, so eventually only the youngest branches at the top that can still reach for the sun will remain full and needled. As a result, space underneath the canopies will open up. Middle-aged pine stands provide roomy, wandering spaces where one can walk among trunks on a deep bed of crisp needles that release their fragrance.

The designers added the element of landforms to many of the plantations, intensifying the spatial experience. In some parts of the park

↑ An aerial view of the large park clearly shows its diagonal organization.

→ A planting plan for one of the woodland blocks illustrates a diversity of trees and understory species within the structure of the ten-foot grid.

↑ Beyond small groves of birch trees in a meadow can be seen the lines of trunks in a woodland block bisected by a pedestrian path.

↗ A band of coarse stone in the foreground and grassed banks in the distance retain the plinths of densely planted pine in woodland blocks.

elevated planes are retained by regularly sloping grassed banks, while elsewhere they sit on coarse-rock plinths. Mown grass defines the base of a plinth, whose steep coarse-stone retaining slope nearly reaches eye level, so visitors can see the level surface where hundreds of trees have been densely planted. The pine trees on the plinth are currently acting as a dark, solid form, separating exterior paths and controlling views. Rather than offering space within, they form adjacent spaces to inhabit.

The stone retaining walls are about equal in height to the stands of pines that grow upon it. Both are equally forbidding. In a decade or so, however, as the pine canopy rises, a band of space filtered by densely spaced trunks will open up between the canopy and the base. Eventually it will become larger than either the canopy or base, since these pines can grow to be more than one hundred feet tall. The elevated plinth will further emphasize the pine grove's commanding height. In the future, this space will invite people to picnic on the plinth, feel its height, and look out to adjacent landforms and tree masses, from under a high, needled ceiling.

The principle of close spacing applies to all of the park's groves. The wooded bands are narrower than the woodland plantations but generally follow the diagonal organization along their length, often along park boundaries. They are planted in a grid and spaced from 8.5 to 12.8 feet on center. Some are monospecific groves, consisting of linden or scattered lines of ash. The lines of these trees reflect and follow farmland and urban plot lines and are also determined by the prevailing winds.

There are eleven bosquets of smaller rectangular thickets whose orientation turns from the diagonal to follow the compass. They stand on elevated plinths independently within the open meadows that surround them. The bosquets are sculpted by both the raised landforms and the hundreds of deciduous trees planted in lines that are

↗ A wall that joins a raised landform and borders the pedestrian spine separates perennial gardens from pine plantations.

occasionally broken and interrupted by low hedges and openings. The trees are spaced ten feet on center, just like the woodland plantations, but in lines that are further apart. The ground plane of these bosquets is habitable lawn, occasionally interspersed with low hedges.

The smallest groves are groups of deciduous trees that break away from the plantations, bands, and bosquets but never simply stand alone. With close but somewhat less regular spacing, these small copses connect the meadows to the woodlands. The close-spacing principle that governs the experience of the groves at Riemer Park calls to mind an encompassing invisible grid that links all of the trees together. Even scattered, open-grown trees appear to fall on the intersections of this intentional but invisible grid.

↓ The pedestrian spine runs through the flat grass plane of a bosquet sculpted by hundreds of deciduous trees.

↘ A line of granite and a line of tree trunks separate a bosquet from the surrounding sunny meadow.

↑ Among widely spaced trees a bench invites visitors to enjoy the view of a meadow blooming with spring flowers.

↓ Distant neighborhoods, woodland blocks, and the beach of the swimming lake are visible from a great mound.

The meadows that surround these volumes of trees and landforms consist of knee-high grasses filled with wildflowers. They are mown occasionally to keep them from becoming woody. The principles of mowing were determined in the plan and the maintenance concept. There is less mowing in the south where the meadows are more extensive but grasses are mown short in places where they are used as lawns for gathering and sunbathing, on the banks of landforms, and in wide shoulders to pathways.

Two great mounds for snow sledding, climbing, and kite flying were constructed from huge volumes of fill from the site. From the top visitors can enjoy panoramic views of the woodland plantations, closely scattered trees, meadows, and the twenty-four-acre designed swimming lake fed by groundwater that provides a shoreline in the pebbled beach and water gardens at the opposite end. On the north shore of the lake, trees planted on upper and lower grass terraces punctuate a five-hundred-foot-long amphitheater that can accommodate ten thousand sunbathers. Though planted in lines, these trees are spaced in a way that is irregular and wider than in the blocks and groves. The trees are still too small to offer much shade now, but their configuration is designed to be interspersed with sunny spaces even when they are fully grown.

↑ View of the amphitheater that runs nearly the length of the swimming lake. A great mound can be seen in the distance.

↓ Water gardens, replete with fish and ducks at the west end of the swimming lake, are fed by groundwater.

What is the long-term maintenance strategy for this large number of trees? Forestry consultants for the project believe that the woodland plantations will be sustainable for their full life cycle without needing replacement. It is understood that trees will be lost, however, and they will likely not be replaced. One exception will be made for trees located on the perimeter of the blocks that stabilize the geometry of the diagonal volumes. Leaf litter will remain in the groves as part of the natural cycle of soil replenishment. Seeds will accumulate there as well, containing the potential for regeneration that defies the grid.

The principle of close planting throughout Riemer Park creates dense forest volumes from the onset. The young woodland plantations might look like tree farms, but there is no intention to harvest them, nor even to thin them. They exist simply to be experienced as they grow into maturity. The regularity of the grid encourages comparisons of how different species grow, age, and reproduce under varying conditions of constant spacing over long time frames. This park is very young now, but when the tree masses are several decades old, their size will carve out spaces that feel sublime.

1996 — ZURICH, SWITZERLAND

Oerliker Park

Zulauf, Seippel, and Schweingruber

TREE LIST

Betula pendula
European Birch

Fraxinus excelsior
European Ash

Liquidambar styraciflua
Sweetgum

Paulownia tomentosa
Princess Tree

Prunus avium
Wild Cherry

Nearly a thousand seedlings that were planted the same close distance from one another create an immediate structural volume in this public courtyard to the north of Zurich. Differences in height, color, flower, bark, leaf shape, and density—not only among the five species clustered within this tree field but also among individual trees—are emphasized through this constancy of spacing. The landscape architects have developed a nuanced strategy to adjust the spacing in future decades that will maintain the collective mass and its geometry while fully celebrating the dynamics of growth, aging, and loss.

When the trees were first planted in 2000, they were so small that they nearly receded from view in contrast to the hefty stakes designed to protect them. Only their density compensated for the slightness of their size. To the new residents, this tree field could not have compared to the green canopy that nearly filled the courtyard in the rendered drawings that had years earlier illustrated the future park. Now, a decade after construction, however, the residents have learned much about the processes of nature: how difficult it is to repair toxic industrial soils, how long it takes to build a forest, and how their present engagement in daily and seasonal processes has superseded the iconic depiction of some former future.

In the late 1990s, the city of Zurich made the commitment to adapt former industrial sites into new public spaces around which the private sector could build commercial and residential development. Oerliker Park is in the formerly industrial area north of Zurich that left behind soils too toxic to move or even to rehabilitate in place. Instead, soils were capped in place by a layer of asphalt, acting like a tray upon which a new landscape was built. As close as three feet from the surface on the west side of the park, the invisible cap slopes at 2 percent, carrying

↓ On a postindustrial site in a new mixed-use development in Zurich, an urban grove opens to a glade and water table in the center of the courtyard.

↑ Bare root seedlings that would typically be planted in nurseries were planted in the initial grove at Oerliker Park in 2000.

below-grade water to the storm system. The cap may not be visible but the park does not attempt to erase its past. The intentional architecture of the tree field that is being grown here acknowledges not an industrial past but surely a present one that is made and managed.

Designed by the office of the Swiss firm Zulauf, Seippel, and Schweingruber, now Schweingruber Zulauf Landscape Architects, which won the 1996 competition, the park forms the civic space of a mixed-use development where thousands of people live and work. Oerliker Park consists of a grove in a courtyard surrounding a glade—an urban forest with a plaza in the center—that links the east and west sides of the courtyard across a street. The seedlings were planted in a thirteen-foot grid, half on lawn and half on gravel around the plaza. They provide a structure that is small but dense, punctuated by a blue viewing tower, a red pavilion, and a long green water table. Common ash is the index species, interspersed with blocks of introduced species—birches, sweetgums, wild cherries, and princess trees.

The slight whips were planted with great intentions: to satisfy immediately in density what only time could produce in volume and to create a structure that would communicate the idea that natural processes are understood in terms of change over time. The trees read as a commitment to the future, while the geometric design emphasizes that such natural changes are more meaningfully observed in contrast to the grid than they would be in a haphazard or naturalistic composition.

At the time of their planting, before the buildings were constructed, the seedlings were supported by the larger stakes that, like points in a field, marked the intersections of the grid. The stakes were removed when the trees were large enough to support themselves.

↓ In this early view the seedlings are barely visible independently of the soil saucers and wooden stakes that support them.

↑ The tree field within the courtyard is planted half in grass and half in gravel surrounding the pavilion and the plaza.

After a decade of growth, the trees have become lines. Although their branches are not yet touching, their canopies appear as a solid form when viewed from between the rows. This creates, in both directions, about seventy allées and nearly as many diagonal lines of trunks. Their close spacing means that the grid is dependably visible, at least for the time being.

Schweingruber Zulauf has set up some maintenance principles for the park that are based on forestry methods to govern changes over the decades. An important measure is thinning. When the tree canopies have competed for light to such an extent that the canopies

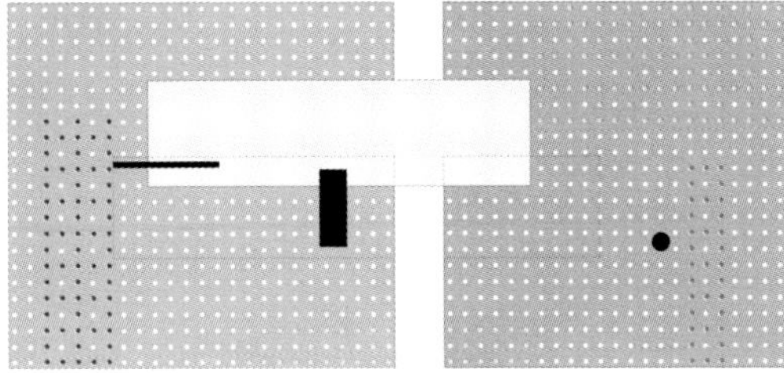

↑ 2000–2005: In the initial phase, nearly one thousand seedlings are planted in a thirteen-foot (four-meter) grid: ash (white), birch (blue), cherry (red), sweetgum (yellow), and princess trees (purple).

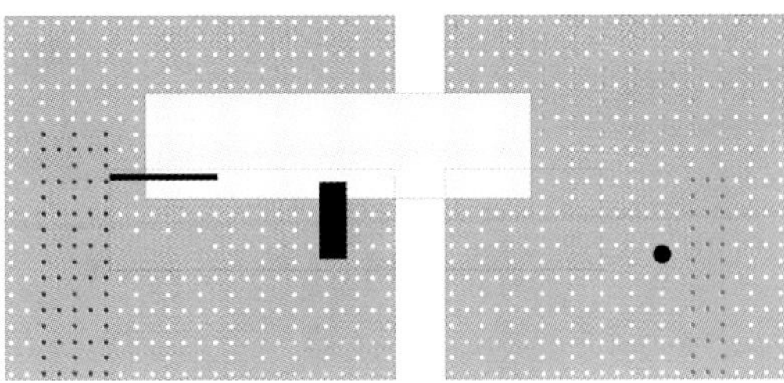

↑ 2005–2015: Adapting forestry methods of thinning, more than one-fourth of the trees may be removed in the first phase to open space for the crowns to grow. By removing every other tree in every other row, a larger grid is formed.

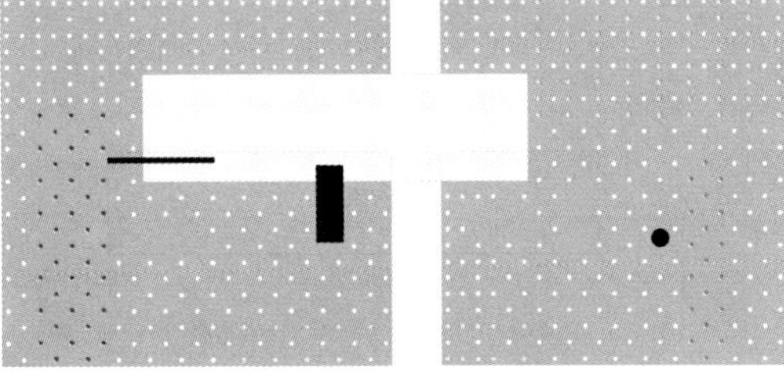

↑ 2015–2025: In the second thinning, 368 trees may be evenly removed from the southern two-thirds of the park, creating a quincunx with strong diagonal lines that merge with the grid to the north.

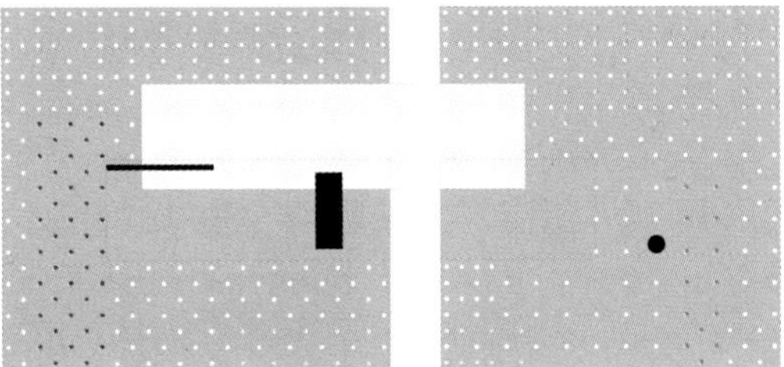

↑ After 2025: The removal of fewer than one hundred trees would create a larger open space at the center and a third pattern of spacing, an open area that merges both with the quincunx and the denser grid to the north.

intertwine, trees may be strategically thinned to improve the success of the overall composition. A timeline strategy illustrates potential thinning in the four decades after the trees have been planted.

Another maintenance principle regards loss: trees that die prematurely will not be replaced. This will bring the dynamic of chance face-to-face with the constancy of geometry. What will the park look like in 2035? The designers' concept for the tree field is for it to grow into a shaded "hypostyle hall," with different densities of a leafy ceiling in summer marked by a tight, a more open grid, and a quincunx of tree columns. In winter the sculptural arching of branches will form light-filled halls. By 2035 the trees will be nearly middle-aged. The lines of trunks, when they become hefty and coarse with age, will always maintain evidence of the grid in which they were planted, honestly communicating their artifice. At the same time, vacancies in a line of trunks or openings in the canopy will communicate the submission to chance that is being engaged here with natural processes.

An important part of the park's design was the selection of species. Three-fourths of the trees are ash, shown as white in the timeline strategy (see page 98). Common in Switzerland, the ash is a hardy tree that should do well in this challenging condition. The large volume of ash trees, and the fact that they are not spectacular as individuals, guarantees primacy to the idea of the collective structure. The ash is one of the largest European deciduous trees. The nearly seven hundred that were planted at Oerliker Park, including four cultivars, were grown in seven locations in Switzerland.

The sixty-four wild cherries came from southern Germany and offer a block of fragrant white blossoms in mid- to late April. They are planted in gravel in the southwestern quadrant of the park, shown as red in the timeline scheme. Under cultivation, cherry trees usually reach thirty to forty feet in height with a similar spread in the open. Because of their shorter stature, the quincunx will eventually form a lower ceiling surrounded by the taller ash canopy.

↓ Residents gather underneath a group of ash trees.

Forty sweetgums were imported from Italy and planted in three lines, with the middle line alternating with ash trees. In fall their star-shaped leaves, glossy deep green in summer, change to rich purple-red tones, drawing attention to their location within the collective composition. The block of sweetgums links and hinges the east and west sides of the park at the southern edge and is shown in yellow on the timeline plans (see page 98). They will likely become as tall as the ash trees but their narrower stature will mean thinning them at a later time. This temporal difference in management will produce a different spatial density that will further distinguish the grove of sweetgums.

In the northeast quadrant, 104 birch trees (in blue) have taken root in the park. They form largely east/west lines. Ash trees surround and intersperse the creamy white trunks of the birch trees that set them apart from the cool gray gravel floor. The proposed removal of thirty-two birches in the first thinning will create nine north/south lines of birches within which a twenty-six-foot grid of ash will remain—likely beyond the life of the birch trees.

A block of thirty-three princess trees (in purple), *Paulownia tomentosa*, was planted in the lawn east of the tower. Before they leaf out in the spring, the trees grow large lavender foxglove-shaped flowers with the fragrance of vanilla, drawing attention to the architectural volume of this plantation.

Today Oerliker Park is thriving. Children are growing up with the trees, playing in the water channel, and climbing the tower for a better view of the area. In the decades to come, the number of trees will decrease, but they will become a larger collective structure, the shaded ceiling of this civic hall punctuated by the intentional placement as well as both the proposed and unexpected loss of tree columns.

← View of the birch block interspersed with ash, in 2009, casting collective lines of shade on the gravel

Seen from the climbing tower in 2009, the tree field is becoming an identifiable mass but is not yet the ceiling of the proposed hypostyle hall.

1998 — GENEVA, SWITZERLAND

Parc de l'Ancien Palais

Paysagestion

TREE LIST

Carpinus betulus
European Hornbeam

Populus nigra 'Italica'
Lombardy Black Poplar

The Parc de l'Ancien Palais is a new public park in a redeveloping area of Geneva that occupies the site of a former palace and military structure, but is now frequented by thousands of students and nearby residents. The Lausanne-and-Geneva-based landscape architecture firm Paysagestion won a competition to design the park in 1998. The firm's concept for this tree garden centers around four hundred tree canopies that form a horizontal ceiling plane or flying hedge, out of which are cut circular openings that project light to the shaded room below and afford circular views of the sky above. The idea was to play with shadows and light by contrasting the tree canopy with the ground plane garden.

To do this with precision and invention on a recycled urban site, Paysagestion proposed a pergola that is constructed from the trunks and canopies of four hundred hornbeam trees, laid out in a sixteen-foot grid that spreads from edge to edge of the two-and-a-half-acre site. The trees form an aerial layer of vegetation that receives the full force of the sun, contrasting with the gray gravel of the ground plane stretching beneath them and reflecting their shadows. In the first few years after planting began, each tree cast a small individual shadow and much sunlight was reaching the ground. Now that a decade has passed, there is more of a balance between the shadows cast, forming a second, playful grid of trees moving across the gravel, and sunlight reaching the ground. Eventually, when the canopies are filled out, only circles of light will move across the surface.

→ Aerial view of the ceiling plane of hornbeam trees, through which a circular pool and lawn open to the sky

The trees were initially provided with bamboo-slatted trunk protection and a grid of cables to support their horizontal growth.

↑ As the trees grow, the play between shadows and light will magnify the contrast between the tree canopy and the ground plane garden. In this view from 2000, sunny areas still predominate.

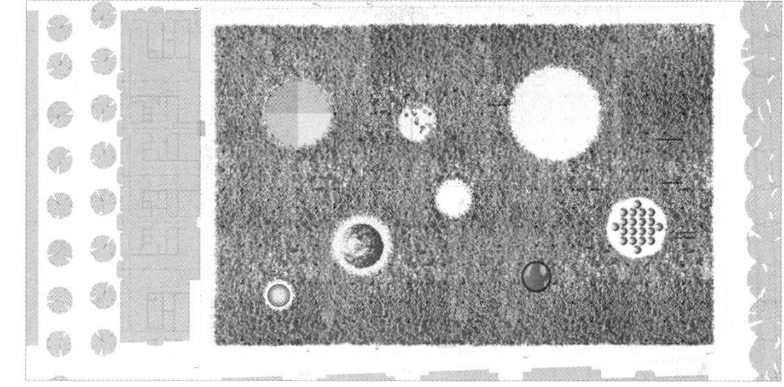

→ The plan illustrates the eight abstract landscape elements that interrupt the hornbeam hedge: forest, tree, field, flowers, sand, water, hill, and pavilion.

↑↑↑ Students gather in the circular lawn area.

↑↑ A conical hill rises from the ground plane of tree trunks.

↑ View of the circular sandbox and play area

Eight circular openings of various sizes are carved out of the grid of canopies that forms the pergola. On the ground plane, these openings highlight an abstract representation of a natural landscape element—forest, tree, field, flowers, sand, fountain, hill—and a pavilion. It appears as if each has fallen through the circular opening in the aerial vegetation and landed on the ground. This unexpected playfulness draws the pedestrian's attention even more acutely to the horizontal plane of the pergola and the sky, with the circular cutouts producing a series of sunny gardens.

In the largest pergola opening, a circular field offers a place to sit on the grass or play in the sun. In another opening, a cone-shaped hill pierces the canopy and provides an opportunity to climb, lie, or sit on it. Another element that breaks the pergola's horizontal canopy is a "forest" of twenty Lombardy Black Poplars, closely planted on a circular lawn with two shady paths traversing them. The Lombardy Black Poplar is a fast-growing upright tree that has quickly become the most vertical element in the park, forming a stark contrast to the horizontal hornbeam hedge. In another opening, a large old tree rises from a circular lawn. A bed of flowers looks as if it had fallen from the sky in one circle, while another is filled with a pool, and yet another provides space for a playground surrounding a sand circle.

In order to enhance the horizontality of the canopy, the hornbeams were initially trimmed up and top-trimmed to encourage their lateral growth. At the time of their planting in 2000, a grid of cables corresponding to the layout of the trees intersected in each canopy, providing support for the horizontal growth. The cables, as well as bamboo slatted trunk protection, were removed in 2003. The landscape architects specified to let the horizontal canopy grow from eleven to fifteen feet above the ground plane and maintain it at this size through pruning.

The European Hornbeam species chosen for the pergola, *Carpinus betulus*, has been known in Europe for centuries as adaptable to hedging and pleaching. It is a deciduous tree closely related to beech but smaller. Its bark is smooth, steel gray, fluted, and muscular, and its foliage is dark green in summer, turning yellow in fall. In open conditions, the tree grows forty to sixty feet tall and narrower in spread. In the confines of a forest, it would likely grow even taller and narrower.

↑ This 2005 photo of the aerial hedge shows the play of shadows on the ground plane.

The idea here, however, is that the hornbeams will achieve their spread relatively quickly, while their height will be restricted. The trees are planted at a spacing of sixteen feet on center, and Paysagestion imagined that the four hundred canopies will appear as one horizontal ceiling within fifteen years. In fact, the canopies have grown more slowly than expected. This is thought to be due initially to insufficient watering and pruning, and possibly to compaction of the soil. Twenty percent of the site is a rooftop condition from the former military construction. It is possible that the canopy will take decades to completely fill in and that the ground plane underneath will never become completely shaded in summer. The play of light and shadow filtering through the trees and the light filling the circular openings will continue their dynamic performance on an hourly, daily, and seasonal basis.

How will the hornbeam trees in the pergola age? Paysagestion has proposed that the lost trees be replaced by ones of the same species of similar size, as much as possible. But the City of Geneva may choose to replace trees with a different species or not at all. The hornbeam trunks will thicken with age and their canopies will become denser.

In 2006 the Parc de l'Ancien Palais was voted one of the fifty most beautiful gardens and parks in Switzerland, a country with an enduring legacy of carefully tended agriculture. The agricultural legacy of a tree garden such as this, with its intentional planting pattern, is self-evident, even though these hornbeams have not been planted for productive purposes. That does not, however, preclude their practical use at the time of their replacement nor the appreciation of the geometric patterns they create in light and shadow during their lives.

→ Nearly a decade after planting, the hornbeam pergola is providing considerable shade in the summer, as this photo from 2005 shows.

1999 — BASEL, SWITZERLAND

Novartis Headquarters

PWP Landscape Architecture

TREE LIST

Betula jacquemontii
Whitebarked Himalayan Birch

Carpinus betulus
European Hornbeam

Quercus palustris
Pin Oak

A CIRCULAR HORNBEAM BOSQUE, a radiating birch quincunx, and an open oak plantation create three strikingly different spatial experiences at the Novartis Headquarters in Basel. The former industrial site on the Rhine River was largely paved and crisscrossed with train tracks, before the pharmaceutical giant commissioned architect Vittorio Magnago Lampugnani to develop a plan that would transform it into an urban campus with courtyards and corridors to orient pedestrians among the company's research and administrative buildings. PWP Landscape Architecture (PWP) acted as consulting landscape architects on the development guidelines for the entire campus, but it is the firm's design for the courtyard and forum at the center of the Novartis Headquarters that draws on the exuberance of the forest within compact urban spaces.[1]

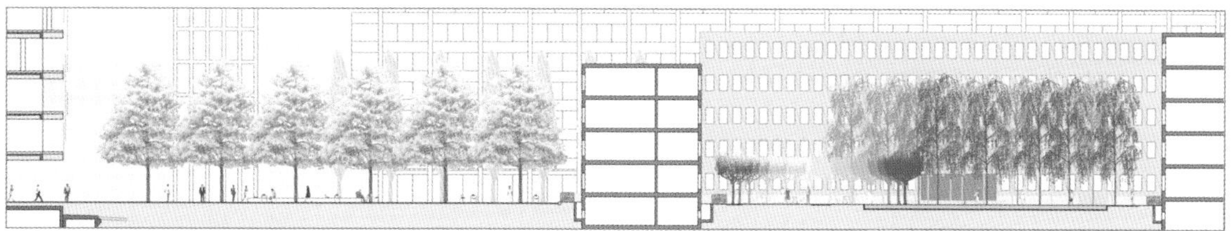

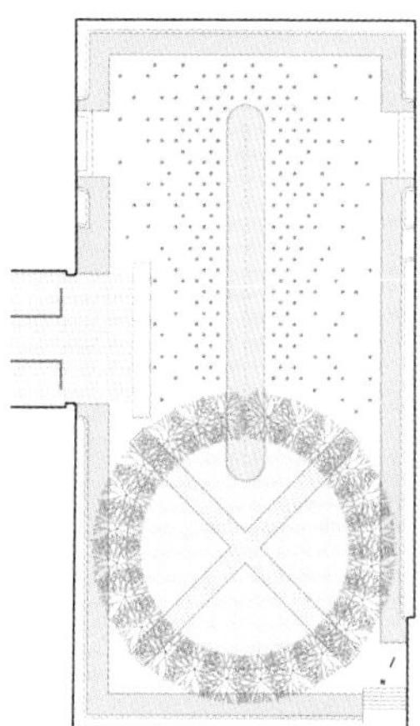

↑↑ A section through the oak plantation in the forum (left) and the hornbeam bosque and birch forest in the adjacent courtyard illustrates differing densities and heights of the trees.

↑ The plan shows the hornbeam bosque south of the birch quincunx that opens as it radiates from the pool.

Peter Walker describes himself as a late second-generation modernist, who, two decades after his education in the 1950s, was inspired through his appreciation of minimalist art to reconnect classical roots to modern landscape architecture. He identifies two areas in European landscape history that brought renewed focus to his work: the agricultural development of the countryside through the nineteenth century and the architectural extension of exterior spaces beginning in the fifteenth century and culminating in Le Nôtre's gardens. Both influences—their spatial organization and material expression—converge in PWP's work in a structural clarity that is negotiated by the vagaries of nature. The allée, the flying hedge, the orchard, the grove, and the forest appear throughout PWP's recent designs.

A sectional diagram illustrates two quite different spatial effects that the spacing and species of trees produce in the forum and adjacent courtyard. Widely and regularly spaced, high-limbed, very tall oak trees grace the forum. In the courtyard, the top pruning of the hornbeam bosque creates an aerial hedge surrounding an open, sunny lawn. This greatly contrasts to the tight and shady condition of the adjacent tall, densely planted birch forest.

The tightly spaced cream-white trunks in this forest are planted in quincunxes that open up as they move away from the pool, forming a tight line of trees around the water that radiate diagonally away from it. Although placed on a grid, the birches can appear as irregularly as a regenerating forest when seen from some angles. Not all of the quincuncial points were planted as it moves away from the center. This variable density of the birch grove contributes to its exuberance, but it also produces open spaces toward the perimeter that affect not only the spatial experience but also the growth of the birches. Trees that are on the edges will produce a broader canopy due to the additional space and light available to them. It is this intersection of precise urban ecology and architecture that makes this forest so powerful, celebrating the renewal of this former industrial site with a collision of intense botanical growth and geometry.

The courtyard is very shady with only a couple of hours of sun a day. More than 170 Whitebarked Himalayan Birches, two to two-and-a-half inches in diameter and about fifteen feet tall, were planted within the small space. The tightly spaced trees in the center, planted as close as two-and-a-half feet apart, provide structural walls for the linear pool, which is open to the sky.

A dense population of trees was planted to provide the atmosphere of a forest from the beginning. PWP's goal is to maintain the collective tree structure for the life of the project. As the birches grow, some of the trees will be removed in order to maintain the collective mass while allowing others to spread out as they age. As few as two dozen fully grown trees may remain over time.

Adjacent to the birch forest is a circular line of smooth, muscular gray hornbeam trunks, spaced approximately six feet apart. They open to a large sunny grassed clearing that is linked by the pool to the birch grove. The dark-green foliage of the hornbeams is amenable to pruning. Their naturally taller-than-wide canopies have long been pruned into hedges. The sectional diagram suggests that in the courtyard they will be top-trimmed to form the dense structure of an aerial hedge. Even if

↓ The birch trees form a tight line of trunks around the pool before radiating away from it.

↘ The creamy trunks of the birch forest form a filtered wall behind the aerial hedge of the hornbeam bosque.

→ This winter view enhances the contrast between the creamy pink birches and the thicker black trunks of the hornbeam trees.

The variable density of the forest produces larger spaces at the perimeter of the grove.

↑ The fall color of the oak plantation contrasts with the pale colors of the buildings and ground plane.

↗ View of the forum planted with Pin Oaks

they are not heavily pruned here in the future, they will naturally grow together due to their close spacing. Hornbeams grow considerably more slowly than the adjacent birches. Although when first planted, they were taller than the birches, a reversal will occur over time. The hornbeams are also likely to outlive most of the birch trees.

In an adjacent courtyard south of the hornbeam bosque is the forum, where thirty-six large Pin Oaks were planted in a six-by-six grid. With trees spaced about twenty-five feet apart, this open oak plantation conveys an extremely different atmosphere from the hornbeam bosque and the birch forest. Pin Oaks have straight trunks and an upright vertical stature, even though their lower branches are pendulous. The trees here are already nearly forty feet tall and their canopies are almost touching. Their crowns have been raised to twelve feet to create an airy, open area for gathering underneath. Like the other groves on the site they are planted in decomposed granite. In the fall, oak leaves turn a deep russet red, which, along with their dark trunks, makes a great contrast to the materials used in the courtyard.

Swiss legislation is environmentally stringent, specifying zero runoff, for example, yet landscape designs such as this one are driven by architecture rather than the pretense of naturalism. PWP didn't shy away from emphasizing human intervention or geometry, as in agriculture, nor from using contemporary materials in the garden. The Novartis Headquarters courtyard fits right into its ecological and cultural context.

← Aerial view of the courtyard

2002 — HUANGYAN, CHINA

Floating Gardens, Yongning River Park

Turenscape

TREE LIST

Metasequoia glyptostroboides
Dawn (or Chinese) Redwood

A GRID OF FLOATING GARDENS OF REDWOOD TREES rises out of wetland in the fifty-two-acre Yongning River Park, located about six miles inland from the mouth of the river at Taizhou, a city on the east coast of China. The soils in the park have been saturated with floodwaters, either permanently or seasonally for millennia, until concrete embankments were engineered to contain floodwaters in recent decades, as has happened in cities all over the world. Although the Beijing-based firm Turenscape was brought in to "beautify" the concrete embankments, the landscape architects have instead designed wetland systems as a foundation of the park that will once again accommodate the ebb and flow of riparian floodwaters. Kongjian Yu, president and principal designer of Turenscape, has described his approach as "making friends with floods."

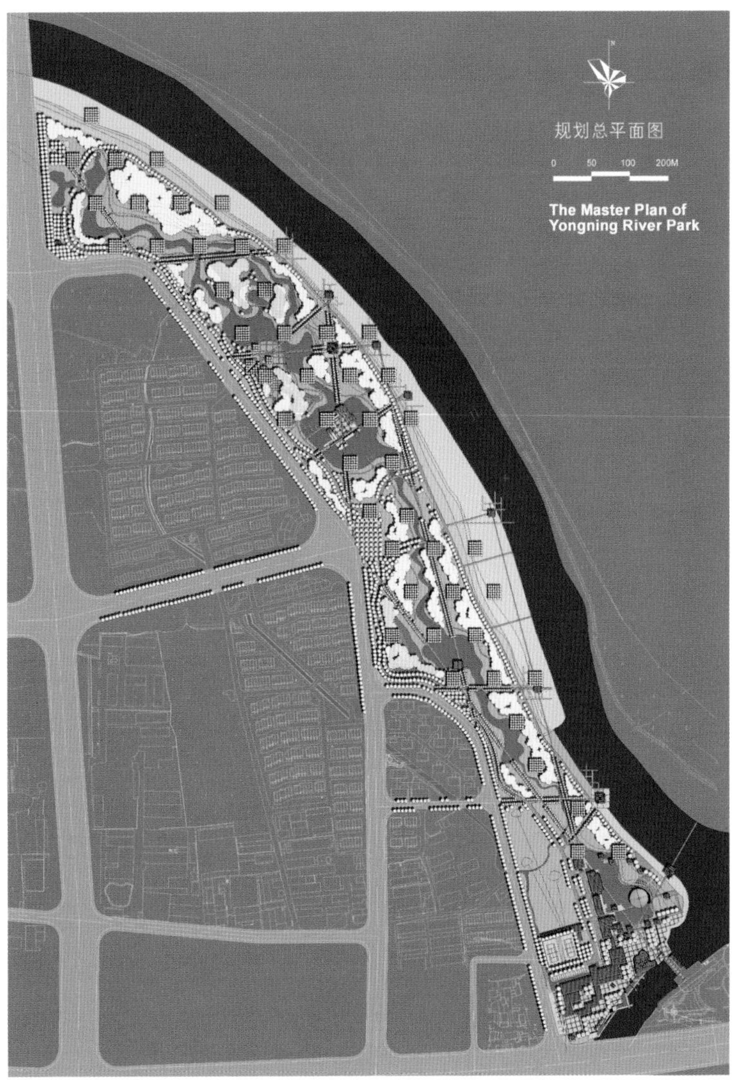

→ The plan illustrates the grid placement of square groves of redwood trees that overlays the wetland system.

The Floating Gardens of redwood trees, located on higher elevations, seem to hover over the wetland.

↑ A path leads through this redwood grove whose ground plane is covered with clover.

As a first step, the firm had to convince the community to develop a regional drainage system and tear down the concrete walls. The design team created an ecological flood control and stormwater management system based on wetlands that provide biodiversity conservation and environmental recreation. As a result, flood problems were successfully addressed, while frogs, fish, and birds have returned to the area and hundreds of thousands of visitors appreciate the river again.

Turenscape conceived of the park in two elevations: the lower wetland matrix and, on higher ground, the Floating Gardens of redwood trees. Each layer is distinguished in function and form. The shapes of the wetland system are designed to symbolize, and indeed accommodate, the flow of water, while the Floating Gardens employ color, geometry, and representation to impress upon the visitor their cultural credibility.

A dual flood control system operates both inside and outside of the riparian plain. The floodplain rises to an earthen embankment, on the other side of which is a continuous wetland system that runs parallel to the river and opens into ponds. During the monsoon season, both the riparian floodplains and the wetland system are flooded. During the dry season, the wetland system retains its water level with additional fresh water, if needed, from the inlet located in the upper reach of the river, ensuring the year-round presence of water in the park.

Native grasses and trees were planted to accommodate the processes of flooding and to create diverse habitats. Though locals traditionally think of such plants as weeds, that perception has changed since the grasses and trees have been employed to stabilize the riverbanks. Masses of grasses accentuate the banks and low hills that contain the wetlands, and enclose spaces and paths within the park. Breezes send waves across the surface of the grasses, emphasizing the power of the wind.

One of the grasses, bamboo, grows like a forest where it was planted along one of the lanes that traverse the wetland system. Already the plant towers over the path, opening to a linear slit of sky that signals the route ahead. Bamboo rigging holds clusters of stalks together that move gently in the wind.

→ A dense stand of bamboo grows like a forest along one of the lanes that traverses the wetland system.

The Floating Gardens that reside above the wetland system are composed of networks of paths, display boxes, and groves of trees. The floating elements become figure to the wetland ground. This contrast occurs in particular ways with each design element. When the network of paths that extend north from the urban fabric are elevated

or become bridges, the experience of floating above the wetland is enhanced, and the idea of the wetland as lower ground is strengthened. As Yu and Mary Padua aptly describe it in their book *The Art of Survival: Recovering Landscape Architecture,* "A system of story boxes is strategically located along the path and is intended to create a local folk narrative including: a box of rice, a box of fish, a box of hardware crafts, a box of Taoism, a box of stone, a box of mountain and water, a box of citrus, and a box of martial arts."[1] The elevation and the colorful walled enclosures of the boxes separate their cultural narrative from the ebb and flow of the natural processes going on outside of them.

The organization of the Floating Gardens is based on a grid of forty-eight square tree groves, which consist in turn of a six-by-six grid of thirty-six Chinese or Dawn Redwoods. Overlaying the site's entire wetland system, this geometry stands in striking contrast to the flowing forms of the plants and landforms that define the wetland matrix. The placement of the tree squares within the grid produces unexpected results: the groves appear in water, on land, or some in combination. Wherever they are located, the squares are constructed on a level plane with the help of retaining walls. The ground surface is gravel or planted with clover.

The Dawn Redwood has existed for more than a hundred million years. The genus was first described in 1941 from fossils found in Japan, and at that time, it was thought to be extinct. The same year,

← An allée of Chinese redwoods leads to a colorful story box.

↓ The retained geometry of a redwood grove stands in striking contrast to the flowing forms of the wetland matrix.

↑ View of a pedestrian bridge leading to a story box, with Floating Gardens of redwood trees visible on either side of the bridge

a Chinese botanist discovered extant trees growing in Sichuan. The Arnold Arboretum in Boston supported an expedition of Chinese botanists in 1947 to collect seeds for planting and distribution.[2] Dawn Redwoods were also native to North America before becoming extinct there some fifteen million years ago and have now been reestablished in North America, Russia, and Europe.

In China people called it *shui-sa,* or "water fir," which explains its choice for the islands in the wetlands of Yongning. Once established, it withstands dry soils yet grows in wet soils. In youth and old age, it is a pyramidal, feathery deciduous tree from the pine family whose bright green needles turn orange-brown in the fall before they drop and leave the sculptural forms of reddish brown, exfoliating bark.

Nowhere near as large as its relative, the Giant Sequoia, *Sequoiadendron giganteum,* it is, however, fast growing, becoming more than one hundred feet tall within several decades. The groves at Yongning were planted in 2002, when the trees were about twelve years old, in a dense formation approximately eleven feet on center. Any losses of individual redwoods within the groves will likely be replaced as closely in size to the existing trees as possible. There is currently no long-term strategy for the replacement of groves.

For the sensory experience produced by its arresting architecture and forestry playing off the landscape's wetland forms, this project won the 2006 ASLA Honor Award, in addition to winning the China Human Habitat Award in 2005.

2003 — NEW YORK, NEW YORK

Brooklyn Bridge Park, Pier 1

Michael Van Valkenburgh Associates

TREE LIST

Catalpa speciosa
Northern Catalpa

Gleditsia triacanthos
Honeylocust

Gymnocladus dioicus
Kentucky Coffeetree

Liquidambar styraciflua
American Sweetgum

Magnolia virginiana
Sweetbay Magnolia

Platanus × acerifolia 'Columbia'
Columbia London Planetree

Prunus serotina
Black Cherry

Quercus bicolor
Swamp White Oak

Quercus coccinea
Scarlet Oak

Quercus palustris
Pin Oak

Quercus robur
English Oak

Quercus rubra
Red Oak

Robinia pseudoacacia
Black Locust

THE EIGHTY-FIVE-ACRE BROOKLYN BRIDGE PARK is currently being constructed on the abandoned remains of six shipping piers along the East River in Brooklyn. The hedgerows of trees that give form to Pier 1's open, sloping lawns facing the river and Lower Manhattan do exactly what hedgerows have been doing for centuries: forming the boundaries of fields—although in this case they are enclosing fields for people rather than for crops. When the park opened in early 2010, the hedgerows, planted in the fall of 2009, were already a substantial structure with a dynamic future.

The park's designers, MVVA, have long been preoccupied with the issue of time in the dynamics of vegetal structures, anticipating changes that will take place over decades. It is not surprising that the firm pays particular attention to trees in its designs, since they

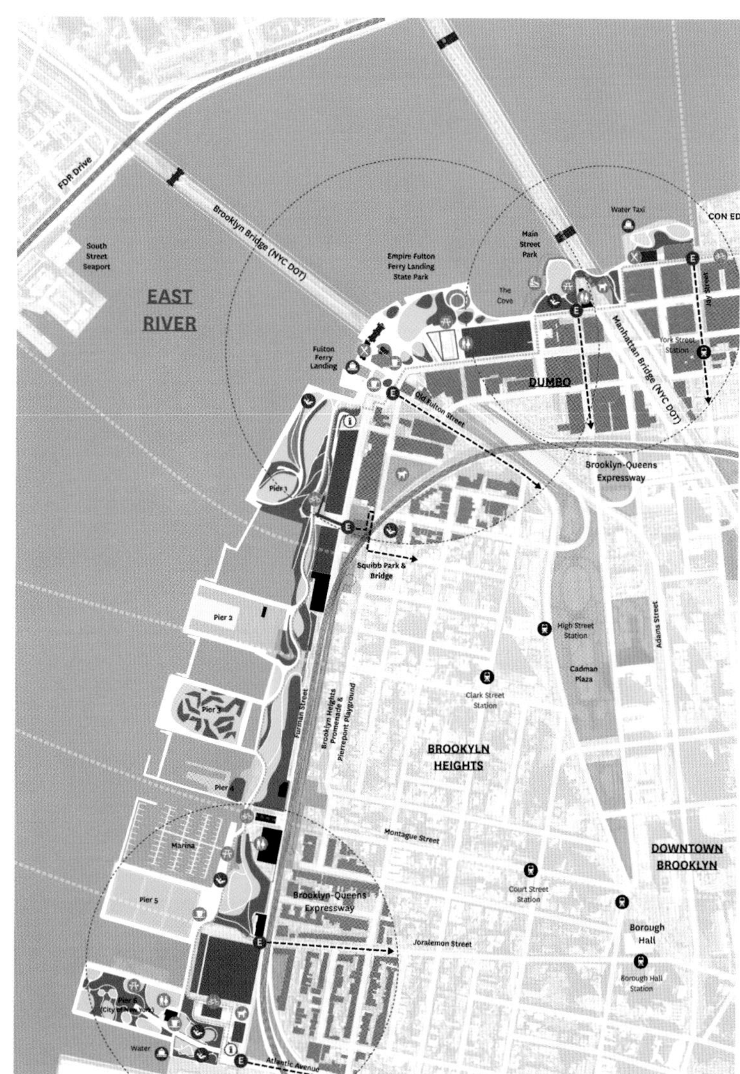

→ Pier 1 is shown directly south of the bridge in this site plan of Brooklyn Bridge Park, which will eventually encompass all six piers and adjacent parkland on the East River.

↑ Aerial view of Pier 1 and the East River with the skyline of lower Manhattan in the background. The Harbor View Lawn is filled with people.

change far more than anything else in the life of a project. "What will it look like twenty years from now?" is not the only question Matthew Urbanski, principal at MVVA, asked himself when working on Brooklyn Bridge Park's Pier 1, but also, "How do you, in addition, provide the immediacy of structure for opening day?"[1] He knew that the trees planted on the site could not only double in size but grow to potentially more than ten times their original size, an issue that radically affects the spatial architecture of the park.

The postindustrial site of abandoned piers, parking lots, and storage sheds that is being transformed into Brooklyn Bridge Park had once been slated for private development. But in 2006 the Brooklyn Bridge Park Conservancy, an independent citizens' organization that has advocated for a great park along the downtown Brooklyn waterfront for twenty years, gained approval for a park that encompasses two recreational water spaces and provides 1.3 miles of shoreline. The projected cost of the park is $350 million with $16 million in annual maintenance and operation costs. Real estate taxes from residential

↑ A path leading through the park is bordered by an open hedgerow on the right and a dense hedgerow on the left.

buildings within 8.3 acres of the project area will be treated as PILOTS (payments in lieu of taxes) earmarked for the park's maintenance and operations.

The site of Pier 1, at the base of the Brooklyn Bridge, has sweeping views across the East River to the skyline of Lower Manhattan, Roosevelt Island, and a host of water-based transportation: ferries, tugboats, and cruise ships. Construction and the dense planting of the park began in January 2009 and was completed the following spring, with the first six acres of Pier 1 opening in May 2010 to eager residents of Brooklyn Heights and visitors from other boroughs and other countries. Pier 1 is organized around an S-curve running north to south that rises and falls to form two large lawn areas adjacent to each of its curves. The northerly Bridge View Lawn's name describes its orientation to the bridge, while the southwesterly oval, Harbor View Lawn, slopes diagonally down to the East River.

Landform and tree groves shape the spatial experience at Pier 1. While the landform will remain relatively constant over time, the

↑ Shade studies, such as this one illustrating the morning and afternoon shadows of summer solstice, informed the location of hedgerows on the site.

groves will change dramatically. The dominant feature of the planting design is the hedgerow, a narrow band of closely spaced trees that has been marking boundaries for centuries. At the park the hedgerow also responds to the designers' goal to achieve habitat corridors, shady paths, and sunny lawn areas on this long, narrow site. MVVA wanted the two open lawns to be as large and sunny as possible, while also providing shade to strollers on the promenade. Based on shade studies, the landscape architects pushed the tree groves to the edge of the lawn, resulting in long linear bands of closely planted hedgerows lining the walkways.

Historically hedgerows were often planted as double rows of seedlings; in many cases they are simply pioneer species that survived at the edge of cultivation or development. The structure of the planting at Pier 1 can be described as mixed hedgerows in its preference for a diversity of species rather than monocultures. Along the pathways in the park, MVVA contrasts two types of mixed hedgerows: dense and open. Dense hedgerows consist of a diversity of shrubs and trees, while open hedgerows mix multiple tree species in a lawn condition.

The firm's planting typology plan for Pier 1 shapes the architectural experience. An open hedgerow in the shape of an S-curve runs the length of the pier. Parallel to it on the other side of the walkway is a dense hedgerow, potentially consisting of Honeylocust, Kentucky Coffeetree, Sweetgum, Sweetbay Magnolia, Black Cherry, Swamp White Oak, Scarlet Oak, Pin Oak, Red Oak, and Black Locust along with a diversity proposed for the shrub layer.

While they are young, the small tree canopies in the dense hedgerows will rise out of the shrubs in mounds that suggest they are merely bumps in the fabric of leaves. But within a decade, their canopies will meet, becoming a singular structure, above and independent of the shrubs, with the tree trunks emerging as visible support columns. In later years, lower branches may need to be trimmed up to strengthen this layering of shrub, horizontal space revealing tree trunks and canopy above.

Open hedgerow trees, potentially composed of Honeylocusts, Sweetgums, Catalpas, English Oaks, and London Planetrees, border paths and lawn areas so that the full length of the trees' trunks and their close spacing—eight to eighteen feet on center—is immediately exposed to view. MVVA proposes that 80 percent of the trees in the open hedgerow be multistemmed, and the designers concocted an ingenious way to achieve this.

The open hedgerow at Pier 1 will ultimately grow into a mass of rare trees, so-called triplet clumps. In the planting hole where one

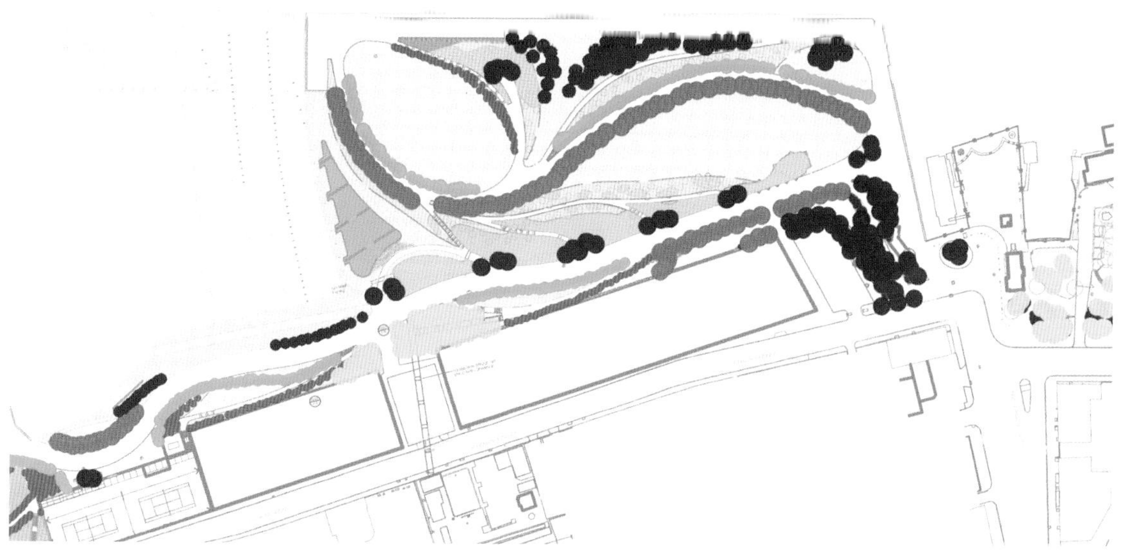

↑ The dark green S-curve of the planting typology plan running north to south indicates an open hedgerow. The brighter green line indicates a dense hedgerow.

tree would normally be planted, Halka Nursery grew three trees of the same species in a triangular arrangement less than a foot apart. This might seem like a perverse manipulation, but in fact pioneer trees in hedgerows often grow closely together along property lines, at the edge of sunny openings, or in other places where they are constrained by space.

While the triplet clumps have easily identifiable individual trunks now, eventually they will meet and grow together into one triple-corded trunk. Each of their crowns will compete for light and, to get more of it, splay out from the trunks, creating an unusually sculptural tree. Their canopies may naturally form a long and wide, linear flying hedge. Although there are plenty of examples of multiple trunks

→ These plane tree triplet clumps are planted as close as eight feet to fifteen feet apart to form the open hedgerow bordering the lawn.

This aerial view shows the parallel lines of open and dense hedgerows bordering the path on each side. The triplet clumps of plane trees in the open hedgerow are clearly visible.

0 Years

100% of total trees
330 ft^3 soil per tree
5 ft on center

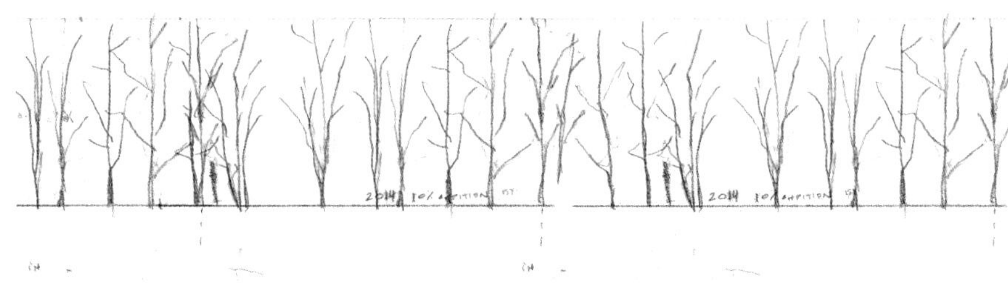

5 Years

90% of total trees
380 ft^3 soil per tree
6 ft on center

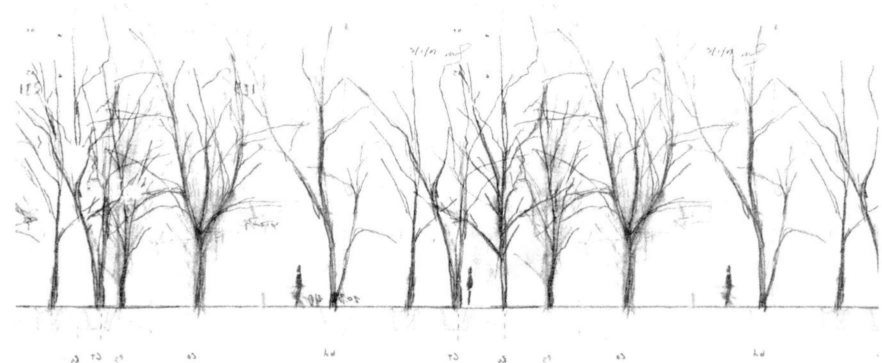

30 Years

60% of total trees
630 ft^3 soil per tree
10 ft on center

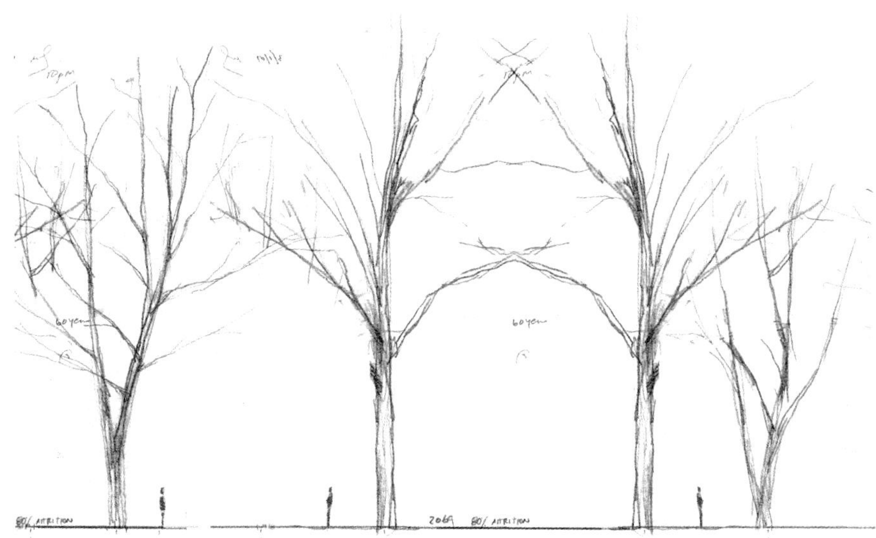

75 Years

20% of total trees
1260 ft^3 soil per tree
20 ft on center

↑ The Bridge View Lawn is formed by the open hedgerow to the left.

growing together naturally in hedgerows, regularly spaced triplet clumps are so rare that their presence in the open hedgerows will likely become a signature feature at Brooklyn Bridge Park.

Though each clump consists of a single type, three species have been planted as triplet clumps: Honeylocust, a familiar urban tree; the less familiar Kentucky Coffeetree; and the widely planted London Planetree. The first two are hardy species with dark bark and small, compound leaflets that give their crowns a feathery appearance, while the plane tree has a sturdy trunk and an open branching structure with cream to olive-colored scaly bark. Grown as triplets, all three species are very unusual.

Planning for Brooklyn Bridge Park encompassed a vision of the project over many decades. MVVA illustrated the life cycles of proposed trees by considering their size, spacing, and soil volume at the time of planting, as well as projecting them five, thirty, and seventy-five years into the future after managed thinning (see page 138). At the time of planting, the trees are, on average, five feet apart. After five years, they will have doubled their height, with a loss rate of 10 percent and a corresponding gain in available soil volume. Thirty years after planting, the trees will be twice their size again, with additional losses and nearly twice the original soil volume per tree. At seventy-five years after planting, the 20 percent of the trees that presumably remain will be nearly fully grown and past middle age, and they will stand about twenty feet apart on average. They will be more than sixty feet tall and have nearly four times the volume of soil available to their root systems than when planted. The lovely sketch by the landscape architects is a generalized characterization of the life cycle of trees, but it is one that thoughtfully envisions how the processes of nature, as well as design and forestry practices, transform the space that people will inhabit over many decades. The dynamic plasticity of diverse vegetal structures has been at the core of MVVA's practice for two decades and will thrive in the years to come at Pier 1.

← Sketch illustrating the life cycles of trees, envisioning how the processes of nature will transform the architectural structure of the hedgerows over decades.

2004 — NEW YORK, NEW YORK

9/11 Memorial Forest

PWP Landscape Architecture

TREE LIST

Quercus bicolor
Swamp White Oak

Michael Arad's proposal for the World Trade Center Memorial, *Reflecting Absence,* was among eight other finalists selected by a competition jury in 2004, and is a diagram for a stark plaza focused on evocative waterfalls within the footprints of the former towers. These two-hundred-by-two-hundred-foot voids, recessed thirty feet and lined with water cascades, would be the largest constructed waterfalls in the country.

A collaboration between PWP and Arad turned the diagram into a human-scaled plaza that has the potential to become a beloved urban forest far into the future. First opened to the public on September 11, 2011, the winning design draws visitors from around the world to the fountains and enlivens the civic space in ways monumental and intimate, welcoming and deeply reverential.

Planting the Memorial Forest in the surface layer above seven underground stories in New York City was no small feat. Paramount to the success of this project has been a long process of negotiation with a massive number and range of constituents who each wanted a piece of the site, on the surface and below ground. Much of PWP's work involved a tireless advocacy to keep control of as much as possible of a nearly six-foot-deep layer of the plaza to create the necessary conditions for the forest to flourish. The substantial grove that covers most of the site is destined for a long life, and it will grow to maturity with many forest qualities while at the same time forming allées at key moments that lead through the wood to the fountains.

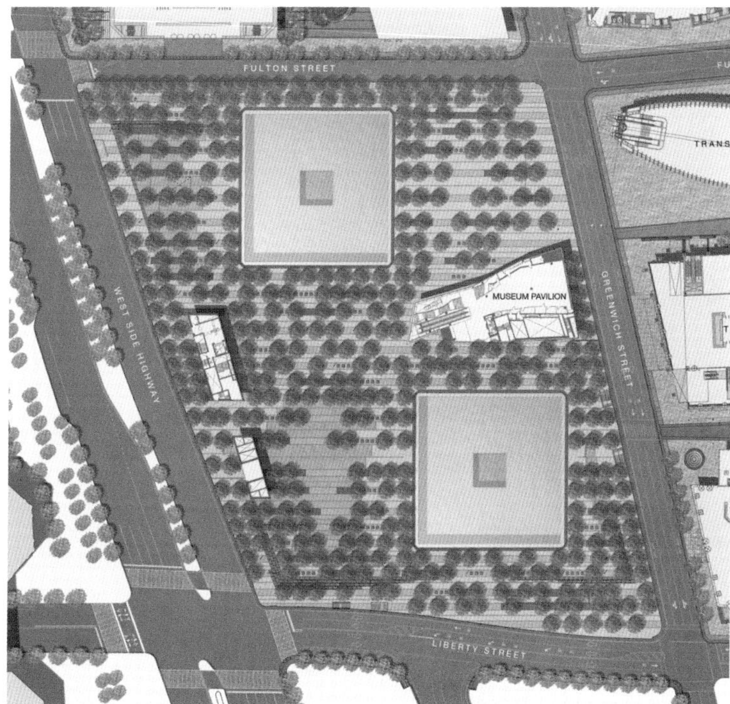

→ As seen in this plan, the plaza is structured by tree lines that form pedestrian allées and lead directly to the fountains.

This aerial rendering of the 9/11 Memorial Forest illustrates the dense oak forest that is envisioned to surround the monumental waterfalls.

↑ Looking across the plaza, the oaks appear to be randomly placed.

The site is an eight-and-a-half-acre parallelogram enclosed by four streets, with the east/west Fulton and Liberty streets running parallel to the footprints of the former towers. Not incidentally, these streets follow the same orientation as the numbered cross streets of Manhattan, the now familiar grid from the Commissioners' Plan that overlaid the topography of the island in 1811, precisely two hundred years before the opening of the memorial. PWP transformed this simple existing characteristic of the site into a generating system that animates the entire project: thirty lines of trees form pedestrian allées parallel to Fulton Street, leading directly to the fountains.

The distance between the allées ranges from twenty to thirty feet, contributing to the forest quality of this grove; the irregular spacing between the lines of trees throws a wrinkle into the perception of order, as does the irregular planting of trees within the lines themselves. This spacing, ranging from sixteen to forty feet on center, multiplies the complexity of trunks across the plaza. Only at particular moments do the trees line up in the east/west orientation.

Although the trees are unevenly spaced within the east/west allées, they line up at the perimeter to confer emphasis upon entering, forming a strong street edge. The trunks also line up at the fountains to create a wall around each monumental square space. At other places on the site the distance between the trees increases to open up gathering spaces: two casually elliptical openings form small sunny glades west of the south fountain and north of the Museum Pavilion, which is also the ceiling for the underground subway station.

The northeast corner of the plaza is flush with the street elevation, while the other three engage steps and ramps to create the apparent flat plane from which the forest rises and the fountains fall. The plaza's topography is, however, not completely flat, but was designed to form slight ridges and valleys, almost imperceptible to vision, that make it possible to drain each allée.

The allées that create a spatial experience above ground also reflect the immediate underground infrastructure that provides the conditions for the trees to flourish. The nearly six-foot depth of protected space below the plaza's surface alternates between continuous structural soil trenches that hold forty thousand tons of designed soil and underground maintenance corridors that are accessible for monitoring drainage and the irrigation of trees. The floor of this six-foot space is another warped plane with another set of drains at low points that deliver the water from the surface drains to two large underground cisterns, located somewhere in the seven stories below the plaza. These holding tanks store the excess water from rain and snow melt and recycle it back to the soil trenches via a specialized drip-and-spray irrigation system.

↓ In this construction shot the underground maintenance corridor for accessing the irrigation system and the soil trenches can be seen between the lines of trees.

Lines of trees become ridges that contrast to the alternating valleys of linear stainless steel drains.

An elliptical opening in the forest offers a sunny space for gathering on the lawn.

↑ Granite cobblestones morph into raised square seating blocks, grass, and ivy.

The floor of the plaza consists of only two materials—granite and vegetative ground covers—but they are combined in complex ways. The tree lines are formed of granite cobblestones that morph into raised square seating blocks, grass, and ivy, while the pathways are made of long, rectangular granite planks, lines of stainless steel drains, ivy, and grass. This structured but flexible alternation of materials produces a rich palette of spaces, from broad paved areas to open green spaces.

The forest consists of more than four hundred Swamp White Oaks in thirty lines across the site and adjoining sidewalks. PWP collaborated with arborist Paul Cowie to select this species for its disease resistance, strength, and longevity. The oaks' lustrous dark-green summer leaves turn yellow, russet, and occasionally purple-red in the fall, remaining on the trees into winter. Their mature habit is strong and impressive, and, in young trees, the scaly gray-brown bark is expressively rugged, peeling off in papery curls. The coarse texture of the trees dramatizes their life energy and acts as a counterpoint to the refined stone of the plaza. Within the oak forest, on one of the orientation lines between the glade and the south fountain, the

→ The course texture of the Swamp White Oaks is exposed when some of their russet leaves fall in winter. The (green) Bradford Pear tree that survived the attack can be seen to the far left.

→→ The oaks were grown in large wooden crates, 7.5 by 9 feet and 4 feet deep, in New Jersey, where each was regularly monitored and irrigated before being lifted by cranes and transported to the site, two at time, on semi-trailers.

landscape architects located a single Bradford Pear tree, *Pyrus calleryana* 'Bradford,' that survived the attack and was nurtured off site for a decade before being replanted on the memorial plaza.

The impressive forest that greeted visitors at the opening in 2011—more than twenty-five feet tall—had been a long time in the making. PWP not only protected the plaza's underground space and specified the most conducive environment for the trees' future growth but also nurtured them for four years prior to their arrival. Large five-and-a-half-to-seven-and-a-half-inch-caliper trees were selected from within a five-hundred-mile radius of the site, with additional trees coming from locations in Pennsylvania and near Washington, D.C., that were impacted by 9/11.

The Swamp White Oak is an unusual landscape species. The tree's two-layer root system allows it to grow well in areas that are dry, poorly drained, and wet, or even occasionally flooded, and it will tolerate significant soil compaction. These qualities and the fact that it is easily transplanted make it a good urban tree, even though it has not been widely utilized in the past. Nevertheless, PWP has developed an eight-by-eight-foot suspended paving system around each tree so that

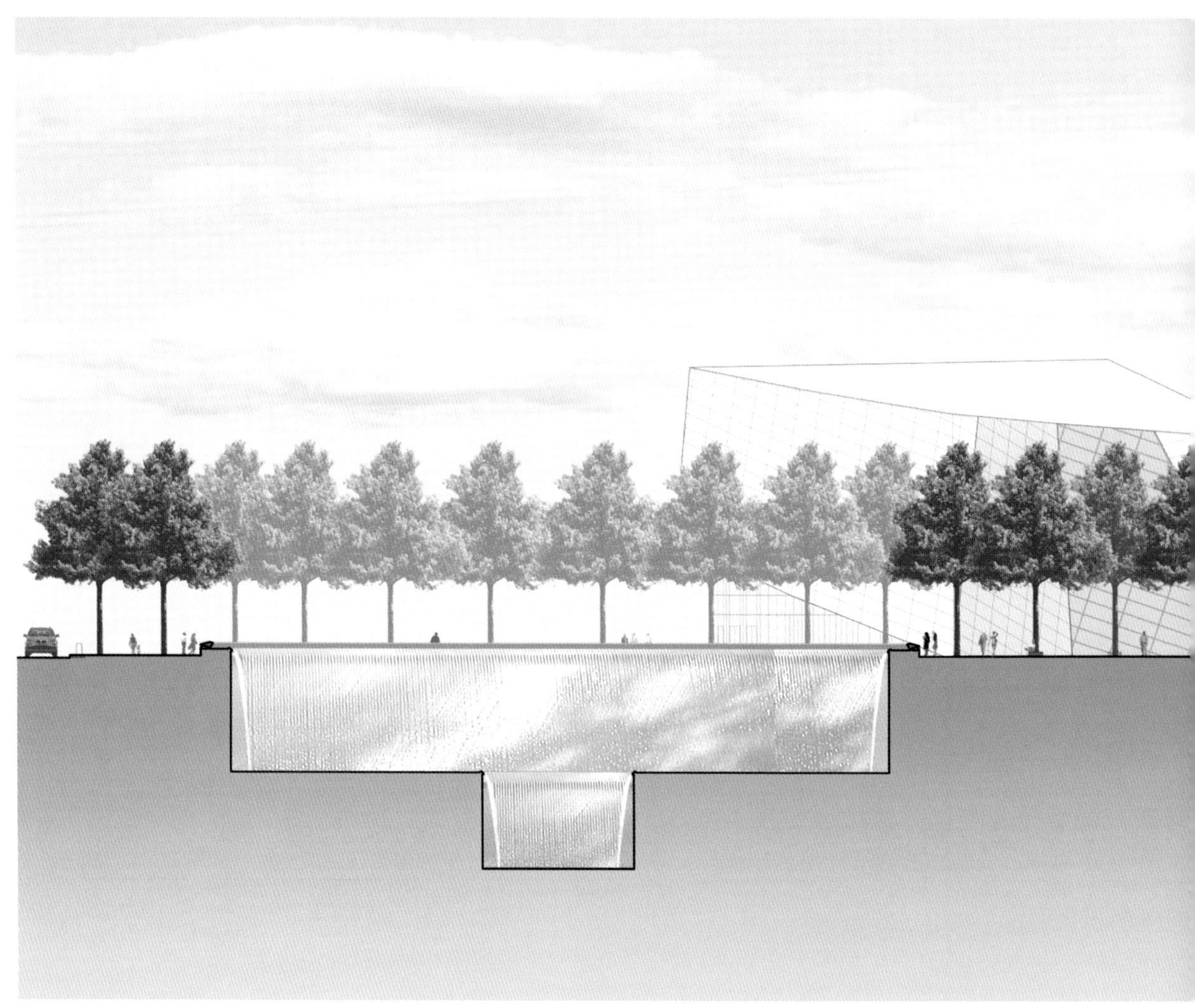

↑ The north/south section through the site illustrates the sky space that will be created in the mature forest by the fountain and the glade.

the soil trenches will not be compacted and air and water can move easily. This structural paving, along with the large cavity for soil that PWP specified for the trees, are the two most important factors in the trees' longevity.

As the forest reaches maturity and the crowns become a collective structure, its presence will distinguish the reverential space of the memorial from the surroundings. At the fountains, designed in collaboration with Dan Euser Waterarchitecture, the trees will function as botanical walls that frame a monumental, square sky space, increasing the perception of depth from the voids at the base of the fountains to the sky above.

Although the conditions necessary for this oak forest to flourish have been so thoughtfully considered that there is not likely to be much loss, if a tree were to be lost, it would not appear as a hole in the fabric, since the spacing of the trees within the lines is not regular.

Rather, loss would further contribute to the landscape's random quality of an aging forest. Replacement therefore ceases to be an issue until the entire forest needs replacement. Swamp White Oaks have very long life spans. This is a particularly poignant quality for a memorial tree garden. The trees planted here are likely to outlive anyone who remembers the day of 9/11, and possibly their children.

This rendering depicts the thickened trunks and interconnected canopy of the mature oaks that will contrast to the sky space of the Memorial Fountains.

The Orchard, the Nursery, and the Forest

The historic and contemporary tree gardens investigated here, though they range widely in size and budget, are outstanding ones. Trees have been planted ambitiously in structural masses, and the designers have given much thought to their growth over time. The care necessary for the installation, long-term maintenance, and, eventually, strategic replacement of these gardens requires a high level of commitment. A question naturally follows: how might it be possible to expand the focused engagement and sculptural experience of such tree gardens to vast landscapes without also investing vast financial resources?

Orchards, nurseries, and planted and regenerating forests constitute large-scale landscapes through which natural processes ebb and flow—though they are far from simply natural. They may be managed for wildlife, water quality, botanical diversity, recreation, lumber, shade, seedlings, and fruit or nuts, but unless they incorporate spatial art, they are neither architecture nor gardens. All three are ripe for architectural intervention.

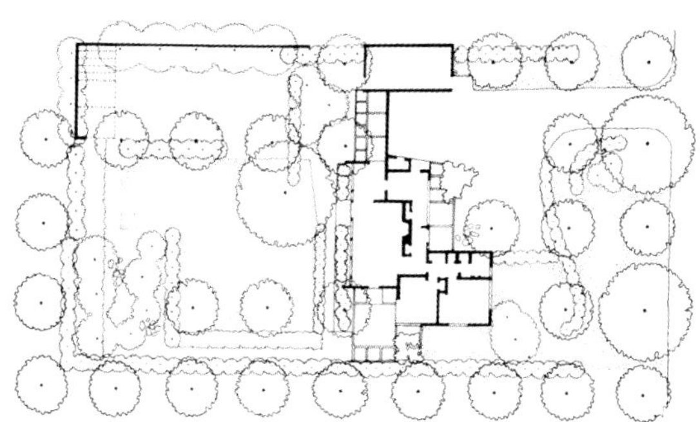

↑ Eckbo's 1940 plan for Menlo Park incorporated an existing pear orchard into the single-family residential design.

Orchards can be powerfully architectural both at the agricultural scale and at a smaller scale, potentially offering a productive element to such public places as parks, schoolyards, and conservation lands. In 1940 Garrett Eckbo was inspired by his appreciation for elements that form the agricultural landscape, such as straight lines of hedgerows, trees in rows or belts forming planes, clumps of trees creating pavilions, and intersecting planes of trees and hedges—to use an existing pear orchard to enrich his design for a single-family residence in Menlo Park, California.

One of the tree gardens in Kiley's 1955 plan for the Miller residence (see page 58) is a small orchard, consisting of fifty-four trees in six by nine rows. In his final plan the landscape architect removed a dozen trees from the center to create a sunlit sky space. This seemingly minor adjustment had radical consequences: the productive grove

↑ Kiley's 1955 design for the orchard at the Miller Garden illustrates a sunlit sky space that draws attention to the apple trees as well as to the space itself.

is transformed by spatial art. The void that Kiley created draws the visitor's perception more acutely to the apple trees as well as to the geometry of the space itself.

Ken Smith Workshop proposes citrus orchards for the entrance and parking sequence at the Orange County Great Park in Irvine, California. Productivity—and its attendant flowers, fragrances, fruit, and geometry—will thus be integrated into the park experience. Since citrus trees have a relatively short life span, even their replacement will likely be incorporated into the visitors' perception of these orchards.

Nurseries all over the world provide seedlings for replenishing groves and forests, but rarely are they part of our experience of the city, the park, or the forest. Vogt Landscape Architects suggests an infrastructure of trees for Dagenham Docks, a former industrial site near London that is being transformed into a Sustainable Industries Park that will not only engage trees as a spatial design element but also continue to supply trees to the site for decades. Parts of the site will be densely planted with tree saplings in small, protected plots. When trees from these initial plots begin competing for light, they will be transplanted to another location on the site rather than being felled. This strategy of an on-site nursery of trees from native English forest plant communities will not only save on costs for transportation and trees but also engage citizens in the process of tree farming, setting an example for other cities, towns, and large developments.

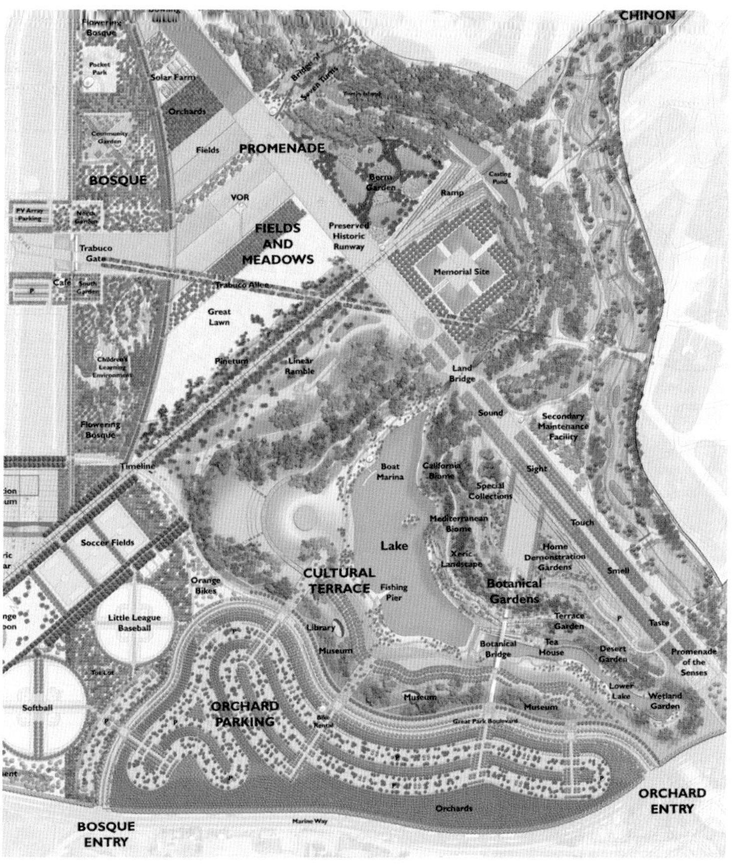

↗ In this 2009 master plan for the Orange County Great Park, citrus orchards are incorporated into Orchard Parking and the demonstration area Fields and Meadows.

→ The Dagenham Docks site is shown in the center of this 2006 aerial photo, before demolition is begun and the nursery introduced.

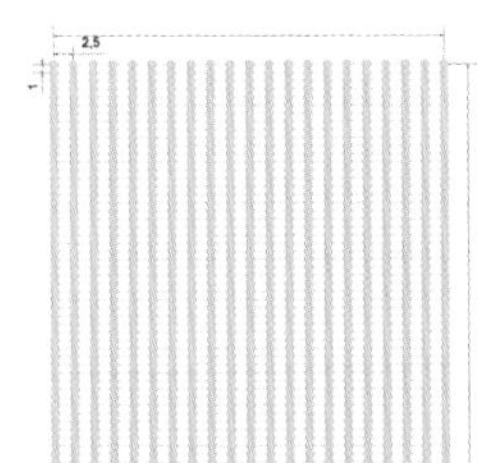

Nursery (saplings)

1×2.5 m spacing
609 trees

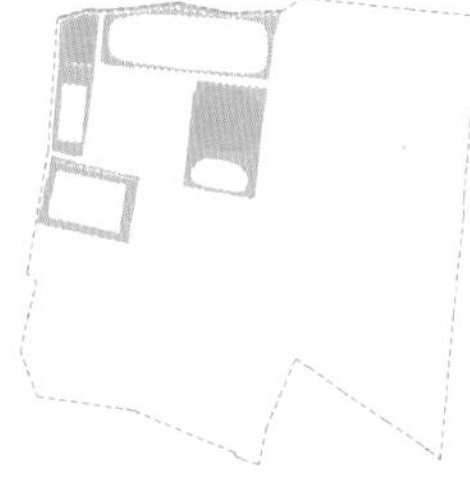

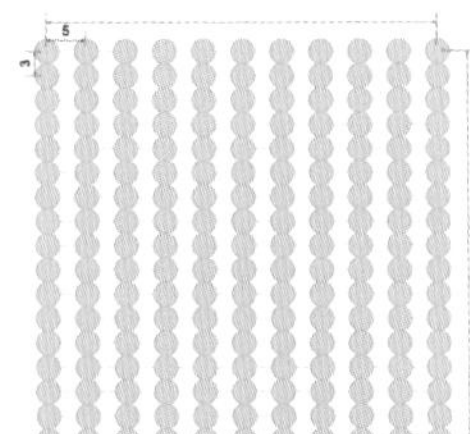

Semi-mature

3×5 m spacing
209 trees

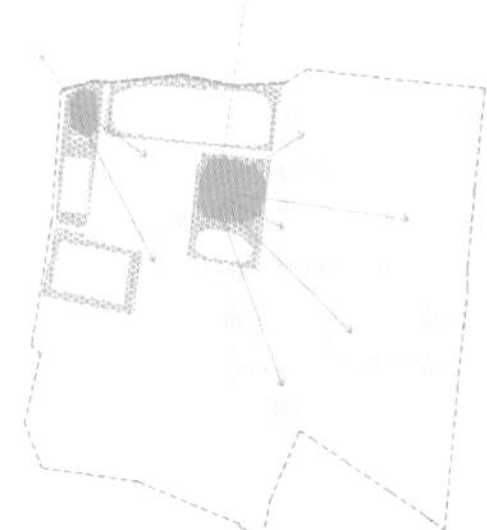

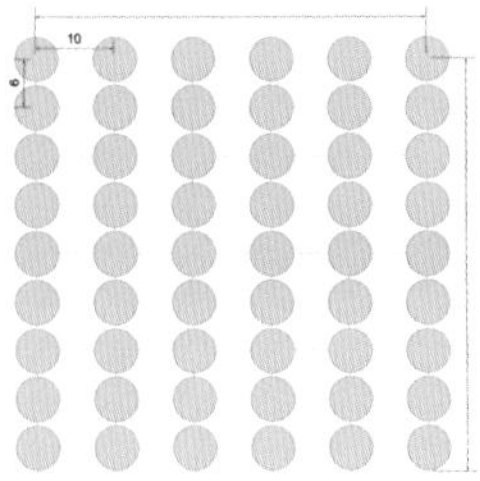

Mature

6×10 m spacing
54 trees

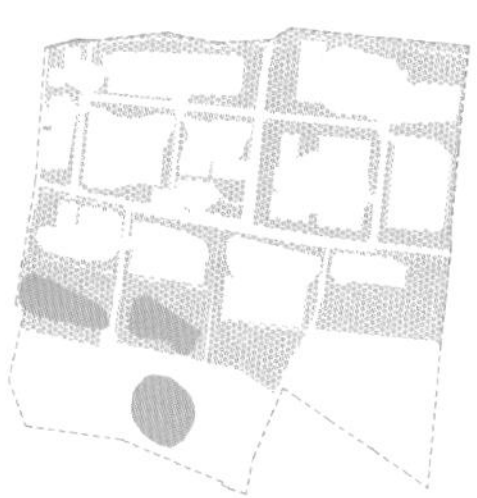

2016

Nursery
Semi-mature
Semi-mature in 2040
Tree distribution

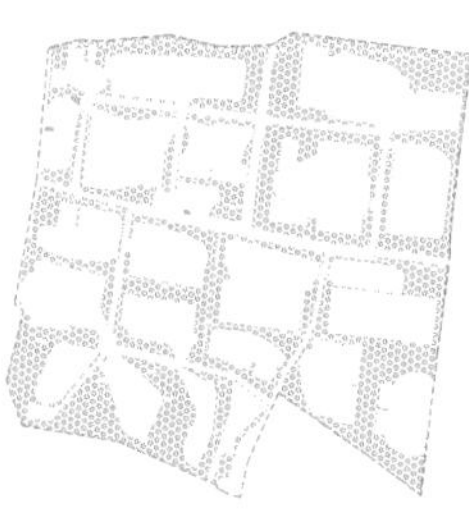

↑ The Nursery Planting Strategy illustrates three stages: the initial close spacing of saplings, the semi-mature trees that remain after two-thirds are transplanted, and the mature trees that would remain after three-fourths have been removed in a second transplanting.

↗ When applied to the site, the Nursing Planting Strategy illustrates areas of nursery saplings (in solid green) from which trees are transplanted to other locations as new areas of the project are phased in.

Planted forests account for only 7 percent of the world's woodlands and range from highly protected conservation forests to the reforestation of deserts in China, the Middle East, and Africa. Like orchards and nurseries, planted forests inherently possess the geometry of the grid, but the form of their overall mass is another opportunity for architectural expression. In Gullestrup, Denmark, a 1968 competition innovatively asked designers to use planted forests as structuring elements prior to the mixed-use development of old farming land. The winning design by Sven-Ingvar Andersson, a former student of C. Th. Sørensen (see pages 46–53), proposed forested belts to provide spatial identity to future development and to protect areas from westerly winds. The belts are about 130 feet wide and spaced 1,300 feet apart to provide space for three to four hundred residences between the belts. Planted closely in rows, with about 2,500 trees per acre, the belts consist largely of English Oak. For three years they were weeded to encourage growth but eventually two-thirds of the oaks were thinned and now the forest is naturally regenerating.

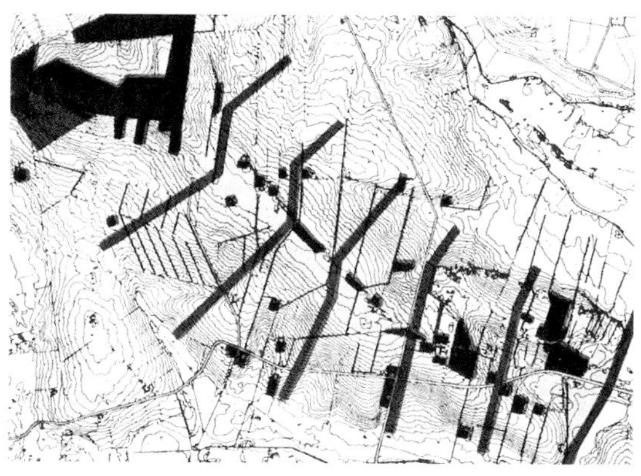

↑ Wide belts of forest serve as windbreaks and structure residential development in Gullestrup, Denmark.

↓ Today the forest belts have become easily accessible recreational corridors that also distinctly identify neighborhoods.

Millions of acres of regenerating forests may not possess the visible geometry of planted forests, but they nevertheless have the potential

→ Plan showing the perfectly elliptical clearing proposed for an urban forest near Paris

to be perceived as gardens through sculptural interventions that highlight their aesthetic, productive, and ecological value. One strategy for expression in regenerating forests is utilizing subtractive, spatial architecture. In fact, for purely ecological reasons, many foresters already create what they call "forest holes" to bring light, and a diversity of species, to mature forests. They just do not integrate this ecological function into the visitors' experience.

In 2005 the National Forests Office in France proposed to celebrate an urban forest in Sénart (near Paris) through architecture. A large and perfectly elliptical clearing—nearly 150 feet wide and more than 700 feet long—would create a large sunny, social space through which visitors would enter the woods. This bold intervention is aimed at heightening the perceived qualities of the forest: the elliptical opening at the threshold contrasts with the darkness and lack of geometry within and affords visitors the space to appreciate, as the French foresters say, the "verticality of the trunks," as light is conveyed from the edges to the interior of the woods.

This book thus concludes by returning to its beginning. In the Introduction we imagined a circular architectural intervention in a forest. In subsequent chapters a series of tree gardens were investigated in which the essence of the forest was continually rediscovered in cities. The final image is that of a proposed elliptical entrance to a woods in France. Here, once again, the ecological and the architectural, human intervention and natural processes are merged before taking us into the forest, the essential source of all tree gardens.

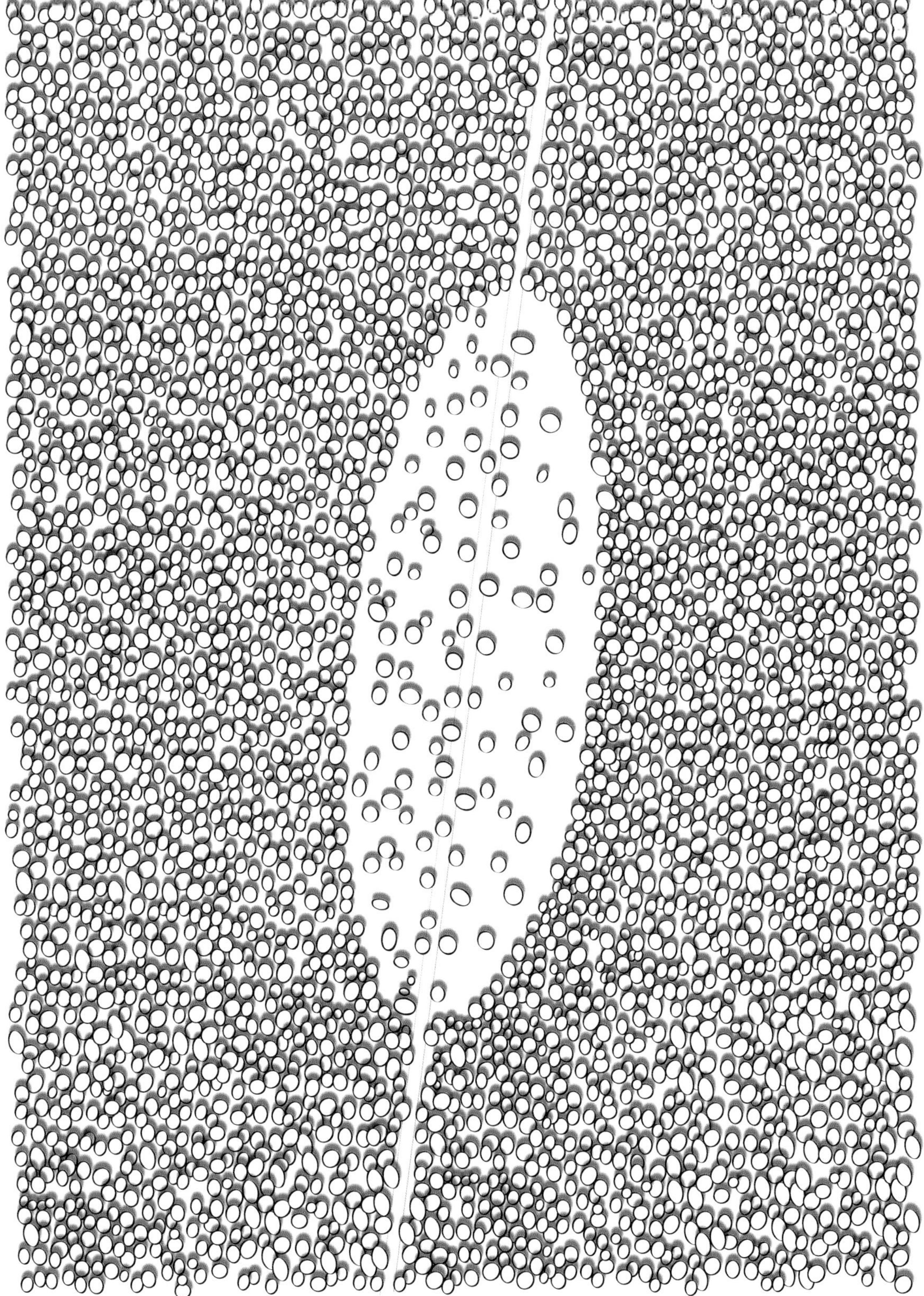

Illustration Credits

All photos not credited otherwise are by the author.

Cover images (from top): Vogt Landscape Architects, PWP Landscape Architecture, author, PWP Landscape Architecture, Horst Burger, author
Back cover: Paysagestion

13–15: Roberta Martinelli and Giovanni Parmini, *A Renaissance Fortification System: The Walls of Lucca* (Lucca: Maria Pacini Fazzi editore)
24–26, 27TL: Scala / Art Resource, NY
30, 35, 36R: Turner Wigginton
31, 34: Réunion des Musées Nationaux / Art Resource, NY
32–33, 36L, 37: Jacques de Givry
41T: Museum of the City of New York
41B: Avery Classics Collection, Avery Architectural and Fine Arts Library, Columbia University
42–43: Museum of the City of New York / Art Resource, NY
47–48: Anne Whiston Spirn
49T: Courtesy of HEART Herning Museum of Contemporary Art
49B, 50: Steen Høyer
52–53: Christina Capetillo
56–57, 59, 60, 62T: National Park Service, Jefferson National Expansion Memorial
58: Courtesy of the Frances Loeb Library, Graduate School of Design, Harvard University
61B, 62B: Matthew Tucker
63, 131, 133–135, 138–139: Michael Van Valkenburgh Associates, Inc.
66: Gordon N. Converse / © The Christian Science Publishing Society. All rights reserved.
67L, 68–69: Sasaki Associates
70B: Reed Hilderbrand Associates
73–81, 157B, 158: Vogt Landscape Architects
83, 84B, 86–89, 90L, 91B, 92T: Latitude Nord
84T: Horst Burger
95–98: Schweingruber Zulauf
105–11: Paysagestion
113–19, 141–53: PWP Landscape Architecture
121–29: Turenscape
132, 136–37: © 2012 Alex S. MacLean / Landslides—www.alexmaclean.com
155: Mitchell Glass / Reuben Rainey
156: Alan Ward
157T: Workshop: Ken Smith Landscape Architect
159T: Sven-Ingvar Andersson
159B: Bo Ulrich Bertelsen
161: Falon Mihalic

Notes

The Wooded Circle

1 The spelling of tree names follows Michael A. Dirr's *Manual of Woody Landscape Plants* (Champaign, Illinois: Stipes Publishing, 1998). The tree lists are complete where possible. In some cases complete documentation was not available.
2 Roberta Martinelli and Giovanni Parmini, *A Renaissance Fortification System: The Walls of Lucca* (Lucca, Italy: Maria Pacini Fazzi Editore, 2006), 13.
3 Ibid., 38.
4 Ibid., 78.

Boboli Garden

1 Claudia Lazzaro, *The Italian Renaissance Garden: From the Conventions of Planting, Design, and Ornament to the Grand Gardens of Sixteenth-Century Central Italy* (New Haven: Yale University Press, 1990), 191.
2 Ibid.
3 Ibid.
4 Ibid. Lazzaro also provides lists of more than sixty common trees that would have been found in the bosco and the orchard, as well as other plants in Italian Renaissance gardens in Appendix I, 323–25.
5 Ibid., 8.
6 Ibid., 10.
7 Ibid., 44.
8 Ibid., 194.
9 Ibid., 211–12.

Versailles

1 Pierre-André Lablaude, whose *The Gardens of Versailles* (Paris: Éditions Scala, 2005) was a source for this chapter, is chief architect of the Historic Monuments Department and has been restoring the garden since 1990.
2 Michel Baridon, *A History of the Gardens of Versailles*, trans. Adrienne Mason (Philadelphia: University of Pennsylvania Press, 2008), 113. Baridon attributes this quotation from the *Comptes des Bâtiments du Roi* to Ernest de Ganay from *André Le Nôtre, 1613–1700* (Paris: Vincent, Fréal, 1962), 51.

Central Park Mall

1 Frederick Law Olmsted and J. B. Harrison, *Observations on the Treatment of Public Plantations, More Especially Related to the Use of the Axe* (1889), reprinted in Frederick Law Olmsted, Jr., and Theodora Kimball, eds., *Forty Years of Landscape Architecture: Central Park* (Cambridge: MIT Press, 1973), 362–75.

Musical Garden

1 Sven-Ingvar Andersson and Steen Høyer, *C. Th. Sørensen: Landscape Modernist* (Copenhagen: Danish Architectural Press, 2001), 62. Andersson and Høyer's monograph is the published work that introduced Sørensen to English readers and upon which, in addition to visiting the Musical Garden, I depended for this chapter.

Gateway Memorial Park

1 Gregg Bleam, "Dan Kiley: Planting on the Grid," in *Preserving Modern Landscape Architecture II: Making Postwar Landscapes Visible*, eds. Charles Birnbaum with Jane Brown Gillette and Nancy Slade (Washington, D.C.: Spacemaker Press, 2004), 70.
2 This long process came to light in a Cultural Landscape Report, updated in 2010, by the National Park Service. The report reveals a process wherein key concepts of a tree garden that Kiley developed in the working drawings—species and structure—were lost.
3 Bleam, "Dan Kiley," 79.
4 National Park Service, U.S. Department of the Interior, *Jefferson National Expansion Memorial: Cultural Landscape Report / May 2010* (Omaha, Nebraska: Midwest Regional Office, National Park Service, 2010), 2–70, http://www.nps.gov/jeff/parkmgmt/upload/JNEM-CLR-May-2010-smaller.pdf.
5 Ibid., 2–27.
6 Ibid., 4–53.
7 Ibid., 5–32.

Novartis Headquarters

1 Peter Walker, *Peter Walker and Partners Landscape Architecture: Defining the Craft* (San Rafael, Calif.: ORO Editions, 2005), 190.

Floating Gardens

1 Kongjian Yu and Mary Padua, eds., *The Art of Survival: Recovering Landscape Architecture* (Victoria, Australia: Images Publishing Group, 2006), 116.
2 E. D. Merrill, "*Metasequoia*, Another 'Living Fossil,'" *Arnoldia* (5 March 1948) 8 (1): 1–8.

Brooklyn Bridge Park

1 Matthew Urbanski, conversation with the author, 2010.

Index